WHERE

—— THE ——

JOBS

—— ARE ——

NOW

The Fastest-Growing Industries
and How to Break into Them

JOE WATSON

New York   Chicago   San Francisco   Lisbon   London
Madrid   Mexico City   Milan   New Delhi   San Juan
Seoul   Singapore   Sydney   Toronto

1 2 3 4 5 6 7 8 9 0   WFR/WFR   0 1 0 9

ISBN   978-0-07-170339-0
MHID   0-07-170339-X

McGraw-Hill books are available at special quantity discounts to use as premiums and sales promotions, or for use in corporate training programs. To contact a representative, please e-mail us at bulksales@mcgraw-hill.com.

This book is printed on acid-free paper.

CONTENTS

ACKNOWLEDGMENTS

The time has come for people to truly stand up and take ownership of their careers. I fully recognize that it is hard, awkward, and in some cases, truly frightening to do so. However, the reality of our changing times dictates that this is no longer optional but absolutely essential. *Where the Jobs Are Now* is for those who are bold enough to try.

This book is dedicated to the memory of my dear friend, Willie C. King. He was bold enough to not only try but to truly live.

I am fortunate to have many friends and sources of support in my life. Whether it has been over a meal, via a telephone call, or through the various means of electronic communication, I thank you all for your support and, even more importantly, for our shared passion to reach our goals and fulfill our potential.

Where the Jobs Are Now was a significant undertaking, and I am fortunate to have worked with some truly dynamic people on this project. Nick Kaufmann is one of those people, and I want to thank him for his tireless dedication, passion, and friendship throughout this project. You are the best.

There are others who worked with me on this project and helped me to further form my vision and pushed me to think even more broadly. I would like to thank Mike Watson, Brian Hartman, Vincent McDonald, John Stubbs, Chuck Mills, Gene

Venuto, Deb Cullerton, Mary Porter, Ed Dandridge, Gabrielle Bernstein, Chuck Ortner, and Robert Smith for their willingness to engage and contribute to the process. I would also offer a special thank you to the "messaging" gurus at Whitepenny.com—Jon Cofsky and Scott Revell. To my friend Nick Kovacic, I say thank you for your willingness to bet on Joe Watson 1.0. I will always be thankful.

The team at PMA Literary and Film Management has once again been my anchor through the world of publishing. I am fortunate to have Peter Miller and Adrienne Rosado as my stewards, supporters, and defenders of my vision. I appreciate all that you do.

A book such as this can only arrive in the marketplace if it acquires the support of a fellow visionary. Emily Carleton, Editor, McGraw-Hill, has been that visionary and my partner in this effort. Not only did Emily help make the book better, but she understood the urgency required to deliver it to the marketplace as soon as possible, and she made that happen.

I would like to close by thanking my family. To my parents, Nat and Marie Watson, and my siblings, Natlie, Nicole, and Michael, I thank you for your constant love and support. Finally, to my wife, Leann, and to my children, Mia, Morgan, and Sydney, thank you for allowing me to share my message. I love you all very much.

INTRODUCTION

What Parachute?

We've all seen the news reports. Thousands of laid-off job seekers overwhelming career centers each month. Thousands of eager applicants crowding into job fairs and waiting for hours in line in the hopes of having their résumés considered. I don't need to tell you we're facing the toughest job market this generation has ever seen. In a report released in August 2009, the U.S. Department of Labor announced that unemployment rates hit 9.4 percent, a 26-year high, as employers laid off 247,000 more workers in July alone and left the nation's jobless numbers at a stunning 14.5 million. The cumulative job losses in just the first half of 2009 were greater than for any other half-year period since World War II, including the military demobilization after the war. During this period, unemployment numbers reached another sad milestone as well: The job losses now equal the net job gains from the previous nine years, making this the only recession since the Great Depression to wipe out all job growth from the previous expansion.

Yet the unemployment rate was even higher than that—16.3 percent, or nearly 25 million people—if you count laid-off workers who have given up looking for new jobs or have been forced to settle for part-time work. That is the highest number

on record since those particular figures started being tracked in 1994. Meanwhile, the number of people requesting continued jobless benefits rose to 6.8 million, the highest reading since the Labor Department began keeping records in 1967. The ongoing rise in continuing claims suggests the job market remains weak even as the economy shows gradual signs of improvement and the Dow Jones Average creeps back up to more respectable numbers.

The number of people unemployed for more than six months continued to rise, reaching nearly 5 million people, a record high. The average time that an unemployed person has been out of work reached 25.1 weeks, the highest reading in the 61 years that this has been tracked by the Labor Department.

Hundreds of thousands of workers are still losing their jobs every month. The recession has cut so deep and lasted so long that the National Employment Law Project estimated that without an extension by the federal government, 1.5 million laid-off workers will exhaust their unemployment benefits by the end of 2009. That's because never before in the history of the unemployment insurance program have so many workers been unemployed for such a prolonged period of time, with some 4.4 million people out of work for six months or longer. Just think about what that means. *There have never been this many people on unemployment insurance for this long before. Ever.*

The Federal Reserve has already warned that joblessness is likely to surpass 10 percent by the end of 2009 as businesses continue to cut jobs in order to stay competitive, and will stay well above healthy levels for years to come. (Some regions, such as the West, have already surpassed 10 percent unemployment, with Oregon reaching a record 12.4 percent unemployment rate, Nevada 12 percent, and California 11.6 percent, according to the Labor Department). Some Federal Reserve officials think it could rise as high as 10.6 percent in 2010. That's

only 0.2 percentage points away from the post-World War II high of 10.8 percent at the end of 1982.

This grim assertion of increased joblessness is backed up by a March 2009 survey, reported in *USA Today*, that found nearly three-quarters of the members of the Business Roundtable, an association of CEOs of leading U.S. companies with a combined $5 trillion annual revenue and 10 million employees, expect to cut more jobs well into 2010.

When the economy finally snaps back and we start adding jobs again instead of cutting them, it's still going to take a long, long time to get back to where we were. Even if we consider a robust and optimistic pace of 150,000 to 200,000 jobs added per month, with as many as 25 million people currently unemployed or underemployed, it will take years. However, the average in a healthy economy is more like 120,000 jobs added per month, and to get the jobless rate down to the more normal 5 percent range, some economists say it might take a decade. We're in this for the long haul, but people need to get back to work *now*.

Here's the hard truth that a lot of people don't want to face.

A lot of the jobs that were lost aren't coming back.

Why? The answer to that question can be found in what until now has been a gradual shift in the United States from an industrial-based job market, where the economy is focused on the output of goods, to an information-based one, where the economy is focused on services. Back around the year 1900, only 3 in 10 workers were employed in the services field rather than manufacturing. By 1968, that ratio had changed to 6 out of 10, and though the growth was gradual, the numbers never stopped rising. However, the recession that began in late 2007, and the stock market crash of 2008, precipitated a sudden, radical shift in the market toward information and service jobs, pulling the rug out from under the industrial and

manufacturing sector with a ripple effect that left no one untouched. In the first quarter of 2009 alone, industrial production fell at a 20 percent annual rate, the sharpest quarterly downturn of the current recession. The factory utilization rate dropped to 65.8 percent of capacity, the lowest percentage ever on records that date back to 1948. We saw this effect hit the hardest in industrial hubs like Detroit, where auto manufacturers shut down plants, closed dealerships, laid off workers, froze wages, cut hours, and asked for federal bailouts—twice—just to keep their heads above water. Unfortunately, even this extreme restructuring wasn't enough to keep the 101-year-old General Motors from briefly having to file for bankruptcy protection in June 2009, or to keep the 84-year-old Chrysler from having to merge with Italian automaker Fiat that same month in order to stay afloat—two Hail Mary gambits that saved the companies from failure, but at the cost of hundreds of thousands of jobs. As a result, the unemployment rate in Michigan alone has reached a staggering 15.2 percent. The upheaval's ripple effect reached well into the white-collar sector, too, as witnessed by the shattering of financial services like Lehman Brothers and Bear Stearns, and the collapse of others like AIG, resulting in some 50,000 jobs lost in finances alone.

People were already having trouble adjusting to the new dynamic of services over manufacturing long before the job market cratered. The impact of outsourcing and technological efficiencies, such as booking travel arrangements online or getting information from an automated program instead of an operator when you dial 411, was already putting a strain on the American workforce, albeit a manageable one. But in the new reality of this economic climate, you no longer have the luxury of taking time to adjust. The unprecedented economic upheaval hasn't just changed the job market; it's also changed the face of

the unemployed. People who have never been without a job in their lives are finding themselves unemployed regardless of their education, the length of their careers, and the breadth of their skill sets.

However, it's not only the unemployed who are affected by the economic situation. A large number of those who still have jobs make up what I call the "anxious employed." These layoff survivors are nervously waiting for the other shoe to drop, while at the same time being forced into difficult working conditions in order to keep their jobs, including increased workloads, fewer benefits, and even less pay. A recent poll by the Society for Human Resource Management found that in the first half of 2009, 15 percent of employers implemented salary reductions, without a requisite reduction in hours, and that 24 percent were likely to do the same in the second half of the year. That's on top of other cuts already made by employers. For example, 78 percent of surveyed employers reduced employee health-care coverage, while 22 percent froze coverage; 72 percent reduced, 24 percent froze, and 3 percent completely eliminated health-care coverage for spouses/dependents; 47 percent reduced, 32 percent froze, and 21 percent completely eliminated employer matching programs for retirement savings plans; and 44 percent reduced the number of paid vacation days, sick days, and personal days their employees could use. The anxiety caused by these working conditions not only creates a less efficient workforce; it also causes an enormous strain on workers' families, personal lives, and goals. According to a 2009 survey by the Human Resources company Adecco Group North America, 54 percent of employed Americans plan to look for a new job once the economy rebounds. The sentiment is even stronger among younger workers. Of those ages 18 to 29, 71 percent say they are likely to look for new jobs once the economy turns around. Like the unemployed, the "anxious employed" are

desperate for stable and long-lasting careers, but unfortunately, waiting for the recession to end might be waiting too long.

Let's take a step back for a moment and look at the big picture. The country is stuck in an economic vicious cycle right now. The economy won't fully recover until consumer spending, the mainstay of the economy, returns to a robust level, and that requires people to have enough income and confidence to start spending again. Yet at the same time, most businesses, big and small, will continue to cut jobs and freeze hiring until the economy recovers, which means fewer available jobs, less consumer confidence, and less income nationally for the very spending that's necessary to get the economy back on track. In June of 2009, the Conference Board Consumer Confidence Index dropped to a cautious 49.3 out of 100 as households worried about the prolonged recession and vanishing jobs. Clearly, the only way to break this economic vicious cycle is to get people back to work.

The problem for all job seekers in this climate is that the old rules of job hunting and career management no longer apply. In today's market, you either adjust to the new reality or get left behind. The golden parachute doesn't exist anymore. So, you're in freefall and you've got a choice ahead of you. You can wait until you're 30 seconds from the ground before realizing that what you thought was a parachute on your back is really a knapsack filled with six months' worth of useless help-wanted ads and empty promises, or you can take the necessary steps to make sure you never find yourself falling again.

That's what this book can do for you. *Where the Jobs Are Now* can help you get to a place where, through learning a new skill or translating your existing skills to a different field, you will be employed for as long as you want, no matter what shape the economy is in. In other words, regardless of whether you are unemployed, underemployed, or part of the "anxious

employed," this book can help you take back your control over your life. Because things have changed so drastically, you can't just cling to looking for a job that is exactly like the one you lost. Maybe there was a time when you could post your résumé on Monster.com and sit back and wait for the offers to come flooding in, but that time is long gone. In today's economic climate, that's like waiting for the job fairy to come and tap you on the head with a magic wand. Well, guess what? There is no job fairy. That's what I call a reality-based wake-up call, and one I've repeated time and time again to the thousands of people I've spoken to as a career coach and strategic advisor. What it means is, you can't afford to be passive and wait around for the jobs to come back, because a lot of them won't. It's time to take control of your career again.

The way to take control is to go where the growth is. It's not hopeless out there, even though it feels like it sometimes. There are choices you can make that will improve your situation. They may be tough choices, but whoever said the important things in life are easy?

It's not just that the growth industries are the only ones that are still standing strong amid the rubble of the recession. There are other benefits to working at a growth industry, too. Chief among them is the fact that you are far more likely to have a positive employment experience at a business that's part of a growing field instead of a shrinking one. Workers are more likely to receive raises and promotions, because when a business grows, employers need more workers to step up and fill the higher jobs. Similarly, workers in growth industries are more likely to have better, more robust benefits packages available to them, as well as perks like subsidized gym membership and transportation reimbursement plans. It's not like anyone's desperately trying to quit Google, right? Nor am I seeing any health-care workers fleeing through the doors of Mount Sinai

Hospital. People want to stay employed in growth industries because, by its very definition, working in a growth industry is better than working anywhere else, and that inevitably leads to a happier, more productive career.

Think of your career as if it were a business. You don't see any businesses out there spending all their time trying to find the customers with no money, or who have so little money that they can't spend it on that business's products, do you? Of course not. A company like that wouldn't last two seconds. Instead, businesses know they need to target customers who've got the money to spend. There's no reason you shouldn't treat your career the same way. Why chase a job in a shrinking industry, where benefits packages are being cut and there's no room for advancement, when you can go where the growth opportunities are instead?

During my 10 years' experience operating StrategicHire, an executive search firm that has helped organizations hire hundreds of employees, and in my time as a top expert for Employ.com, I've met a lot of people and helped them find a lot of jobs, from CXO positions to senior management executives, board of director members, and beyond. I've advised workers throughout the nation on how to get back on their feet and find satisfying, long-lasting, and lucrative careers.

I speak extensively all over the country on the topics of human capital strategies, personal development, employment opportunities, and the economy. Not too long ago at one of these speaking engagements, I met a man who had lost his job and was at the end of his rope. He said to me, "Joe, at this point I'll do whatever it takes to find work."

I said, "Move to Texas. Right now Austin, San Antonio, and Houston have lower unemployment rates than the rest of the country."

He made a face and replied, "Oh, I don't want to move to *Texas*."

I told him, "Then you aren't really willing to do whatever it takes, are you?"

Like I said, there are tough choices to make. But luckily, they're not choices you have to make blindly. You just need to know where to look.

There are still plenty of growth industries out there just waiting for qualified workers. *Where the Jobs Are Now* will show you what those fields are, and break down the industries and roles in a clear, down-to-earth way for workers looking to embark on the next part of their careers. At the back of the book, you'll find an appendix that will act as your one-stop guide to career resources for each of the industries we'll be covering in the chapters ahead, including career news and job sites, and information on grants, scholarships, and loans you can apply for while learning a new skill.

It's easy to get overwhelmed by all the doom-and-gloom numbers being reported in the news every day. It's also easy to get overwhelmed when presented with a multitude of career options like the ones you'll find in this book. So it's important to remember amid all the noise and numbers that, in the end, you're only looking for one job.

Yours.

Where the Jobs Are Now can help. This is your complete resource and reference guide to the career that's waiting for you.

In a job market that oftentimes feels hopeless, *Where the Jobs Are Now* can be your pathway to hope.

CHAPTER 1

HEALTH CARE

Even in the worst economic climate, there are certain constants you can count on. Among them is the fact that people will still get sick, people will still get hurt, and people will still grow old. Certainly no one is going to stop aging or catching colds just because the Dow dropped another 600 points. As long as people continue to have health needs, they are going to require an industry to take care of them.

As health care continues to evolve with technological advances and clinical developments, Americans are generally living longer than ever before. In the United States alone, 13,000 individuals are expected to turn 60 each day over the next 20 years. With our aging population requiring more and more health care, advances in medical technology that have improved the survival rates of trauma victims and the severely ill, and retiring baby boomers projected to leave thousands of vacancies in the field over the next 10 years, opportunities in the health-care industry aren't drying up anytime soon. In fact, in February 2009, while the recession was cutting away another 650,000 jobs, employment in health care actually *grew* by 30,000 jobs. According to the Department of Labor, some 413,000 jobs were added to the field over the 12-month period between May 2008 and April 2009, and there are no signs of this growth stopping.

Because of our nation's increasing needs, health care has become the single largest industry in the United States. With the consideration of the professional workforce and the ancillary jobs within the industry, it's estimated that 1 in every 11 U.S. residents works in the health-care business. Furthermore, the need for more workers is increasing so drastically that health care is expected to generate 3,000,000 new jobs by 2016, more than any other industry.

The face of the health-care industry is one everybody knows well: doctors, nurses, ambulance drivers, hospital staff, and so on. Yet within the industry, there are actually hundreds of different roles that need to be filled in order to keep up with the growing demand for health care, roles that can be found within the approximately 580,000 establishments across the country that compose the health-care industry.

The best known and most visible health-care establishment is, of course, the hospital. Every year, hospitals provide vital health-care services for an estimated 700 million people, services that include everything from emergency care to surgery to delivering babies. As a result, hospital care makes up the largest component of the health-care sector. With the industry in total representing about 16 percent of the gross domestic product (GDP)—a measure of economic output—or approximately $2.1 trillion, hospitals alone account for $648 billion of that total. With numbers like these, it's easy to see why the health-care industry is an economic mainstay, providing stability and growth even during times of recession.

A report by the American Hospital Association in 2006 concluded that hospitals are among the largest employers in many communities, employing more than 5 million people and spending about $286 billion on goods and services in addition to employee wages. Taken on a national scale, this

means each hospital job actually supports almost two additional jobs, and every dollar spent by a hospital supports more than $2 of additional business activity. Counting these ripple-effect benefits to the community, hospitals support nearly $1.9 trillion of economic activity across the United States. This makes hospitals not only a large, established source of employment providing jobs for a wide range of skill levels, but it also makes hospitals a stable source of employment growth despite economic turmoil. Hospitals employ workers with all levels of education and training, from highly skilled physicians, surgeons, nurses, therapists, and social workers to lower-skilled workers in a variety of support positions. Roughly 3 out of every 10 hospital employees are registered nurses, while about 1 out of 5 employees are in a service occupation, such as nurses' assistants, psychiatric care staff, and home health aides. Earnings of hospital workers, on average, tend to be higher than those of workers in most other sectors of the service industry. Additionally, hospitals also furnish benefits like health insurance that are often lacking in other jobs available to lower-skilled workers, such as retail or other service jobs.

Facing a shortage of skilled workers, hospitals are currently investing in workforce development and retention activities. Some hospitals offer tuition reimbursement programs, partner with local colleges to provide training programs for employees to update or develop their skills, or implement mentoring programs for less experienced staff.

It might surprise you to learn that although hospitals employ 34.8 percent of all health-care workers, they only constitute about 1 percent of all health-care establishments. An amazing 87.1 percent of health-care establishments are actually the smaller, more widely distributed establishments that when taken together are known as ambulatory health-care services.

These establishments collectively employ 42.2 percent of workers in the industry, even more than hospitals. They include the following:

- Physicians' offices, which employ 17.1 percent of workers in the industry. Many of the jobs in these offices are in professional and related occupations, primarily physicians, surgeons, and registered nurses. However, about two out of every five jobs in physicians' offices are in administrative support occupations, such as receptionists and information clerks.
- Home health-care services employ 6.9 percent, primarily registered nurses, physical therapists, home health aides, and personal and home-care aides to provide skilled nursing and medical care in the home for the elderly and infirm.
- Dentists' offices employ 6.3 percent, primarily dental hygienists and dental assistants. With demand for dental care on the rise due to population growth and a greater retention of natural teeth by the middle-aged and elderly, larger practices are more likely to employ office managers and administrative support workers as well as to help meet their increased workloads.
- Other health practitioners' offices—such as chiropractors, optometrists, podiatrists, occupational and physical therapists, psychologists, audiologists, speech-language pathologists, dietitians, acupuncturists, homeopaths, and hypnotherapists—employ 4.6 percent. While two in five jobs here are professional and related occupations, office managers and technical and administrative support positions make up the rest.
- Outpatient care centers, which include diverse establishments like kidney dialysis centers, outpatient

mental health and substance abuse centers, HMO (health maintenance organization) medical centers, clinics, and freestanding ambulatory surgical and emergency centers, employ 3.9 percent, mostly counselors, social workers, and registered nurses.

- Other ambulatory health-care services, composed of everything from ambulance and helicopter transport services, to blood and organ banks, to pacemaker monitoring services and smoking cessation programs, employ 1.7 percent of the industry, approximately half of which are emergency medical technicians (EMTs), paramedics, and ambulance drivers and attendants.

- Medical and diagnostic laboratories, which provide supplemental services like analyzing blood or taking X rays, employ 1.6 percent of the industry. Professional and related workers, primarily clinical laboratory and radiologic technologists and technicians, are joined here by services workers such as medical assistants, medical equipment preparers, and medical transcriptionists.

After hospitals and ambulatory health-care services, the remaining 23 percent of employment in the health-care industry comes from nursing and residential care facilities. About two out of three jobs in these facilities are in service occupations, primarily nursing, psychiatric counseling, and home health aides—a much higher ratio of service workers to professionals than exists in other health-care establishments. Because federal law requires all nursing facilities to have licensed personnel on hand 24 hours a day in order to maintain an appropriate level of care, these establishments tend to employ large groups of workers. These establishments include the following:

- Nursing care facilities, which provide inpatient nursing, rehabilitation, and health-related personal care to those who need continuous nursing care but do not require hospital services, employ 12.6 percent of health-care workers.
- Community care facilities for the elderly, which employ 5 percent.
- Residential mental health facilities, which employ 4 percent.
- Other residential care facilities, such as alcohol and drug rehabilitation centers, group homes, and halfway houses, which employ 1.3 percent.

Employment in the health-care industry will continue to boom for several reasons. The number of people in older age groups, with much greater than average health-care needs, is projected to grow faster than the total population by 2016, and as a result, the demand for health care will only increase. Employment in home health care, nursing, and residential care will also increase rapidly as life expectancies rise, and as aging children are less able to care for their parents and rely more on long-term care facilities. Advances in medical technology will continue to improve the survival rate of severely ill and injured patients, who will then need extensive physical therapy and recovery care. New technologies are also making it possible to identify and treat conditions that were previously untreatable. Medical group practices and integrated health systems are poised to become larger and more complex, increasing the need for office and administrative support workers. Industry growth will also occur as a result of the shift from inpatient to less expensive outpatient and home health care, thanks to improvements in diagnostic testing and surgical procedures, as well as an increasing number of patients who wish to be treated at home.

Not that this means you have to rush off to medical school for four years to pursue an expensive M.D. degree. There are plenty of opportunities available that you can take advantage of a lot faster and without having to make an enormous monetary investment. Your existing skills could translate quite easily to a job in the health-care industry, as the field has a constant need for professionals with diverse backgrounds, including accounting, management, finance, communications, law, science, administrative services, and information technology, particularly now with President Obama's push to get health-care records digitized, which could create as many as 50,000 new tech jobs. Opportunities also exist for workers in custodial, non-emergency patient transport, and food services roles, especially in hospitals and larger health-care establishments.

If you *are* looking to learn new skills and become a licensed health-care professional, there's good news on two fronts. First, grants totaling nearly $50 million are being funded across the nation to help workers prepare for careers in the health-care industry. Second, many of the occupations projected to grow the fastest in the economy are concentrated in the health-care industry. For example, total employment of home health aides—including the self-employed—is projected to increase by 49 percent in the next six years. Medical assistants are projected to grow by 35 percent, physical therapy assistants by 32 percent, and physicians' assistants by 27 percent.

According to the Council on Physician and Nurse Supply, an independent consortium of health-care leaders based out of the University of Pennsylvania, the demand for registered nurses (RNs) is the fastest growing in the industry. An estimated 30,000 RNs are needed to enter the workforce each year to meet the nation's growing health-care needs. However, as

the median age of registered nurses increases, not enough younger workers are replacing them, and as a result, employers in some parts of the country are reporting difficulties in attracting and retaining nurses. The imbalance between the supply and demand for qualified workers should spur efforts to attract and retain qualified registered nurses, including higher pay and subsidized training.

As our nation's populace continues to age, the need for physical therapists, especially in the home-care field, is also booming. Employment for physical therapists is expected to grow an astonishing 27 percent in the next six years. In addition to the aging population, this growth is also spurred by the impending retirement and age-related health issues of the baby boomer generation, increasing numbers of children who will need physical therapy as technological advances save the lives of a larger proportion of newborns with severe birth defects, a higher percentage than ever before of trauma victim survival, and advances in medical technology that will permit the treatment of an increasing number of disabling conditions that were untreatable in the past. Assisting in the rapid growth of this occupation is that fact that in order to keep expenses low, some hospitals and doctors are referring their patients to outside physical therapy centers instead of performing the therapy in-house, as well as the fact that insurance companies are now required by law not to limit the coverage for physical therapy claims.

Opportunities for physical therapists exist both in and out of the hospital setting, extending to clinics, rehabilitation centers, nursing homes, sports medicine facilities, adult daycare facilities, outpatient care centers, wellness centers, doctors' offices, schools, research centers, privately owned physical therapy businesses, and self-employment.

Related Growth Industries

A variety of supplemental occupations and industries are also riding the health-care boom to increased growth, serving the needs of health-care workers and patients alike.

Pharmacists

Chief among the related growth occupations are pharmacists. One side effect of the general populace living longer is an increasing number of middle-aged and elderly people who rely on prescription drugs. As the use of prescription drugs increases, the demand for pharmacists is growing in a variety of practice settings, such as community pharmacies, hospital pharmacies, and mail-order pharmacies. As the population continues to age, assisted living facilities and home-care organizations are also seeing particularly rapid growth in the need for pharmacists. According to the Bureau of Labor Statistics, this increased demand will drive employment of pharmacists to grow by an estimated 22 percent over the next six years.

Not all pharmacists stand behind a counter and hand out pills. Some cost-conscious insurers, in an attempt to improve preventative care, are making use of pharmacists in areas such as patient education and vaccination administration. Similarly, managed-care organizations are hiring pharmacists to analyze trends in medication use and to study the cost and benefit analysis of different drug therapies. New pharmacist jobs are also being created all the time in disease management—the development of new methods for curing and controlling diseases—and in pharmacy informatics, which is the application of computers to the storage, retrieval, and analysis of drug and prescription information in order to ensure pharmacists make the best possible decisions about drug therapies.

Medical Equipment and Supplies

Another industry being lifted along with health care, especially as new technologies and treatments are developed, is the medical equipment and supplies field. Roughly 15,000 companies across the nation currently employ some 423,000 workers to design, manufacture, sell, and distribute medical instruments, lab apparatus, dialysis equipment, prosthetic appliances, machinery—even low-tech supplies like syringes, catheters, and bandages. Home delivery of medical supplies is on the rise as well. No matter the state of the economy, people will always need their diabetic testing supplies, ostomy supplies, and pain management products delivered to them.

This $100-plus billion industry also happens to be one of the country's largest export industries, with an additional estimated $14 billion in international sales. This too will only increase as the world's population continues to live longer and have more health-care needs.

As the inherent demand for health care continues to grow, so will the demand for the tools and technologies through which health care is administered. As the medical equipment field expands, it is poised to increase job opportunities for everyone from office professionals, engineers, mechanics, and manufacturers to sales reps, customer service professionals, and delivery and installation personnel.

Taken as a whole, the health-care industry offers a stable and lucrative source of employment with a consistently growing need for new, qualified personnel. Furthermore, as our nation's health needs increase and evolve, health care will remain a thriving career opportunity well into the future. In the appendix, you'll find a comprehensive list of health-care career resources, including certification courses, industry news, and job sites, and information on how to apply for related grants, scholarships, and loans.

MAKING THE TRANSITION: HEALTH CARE

Jamie M., 39, of Denver, Colorado, is a registered nurse employed by a state university hospital, but it was actually the leisure and hospitality industry that first caught her attention. "I earned my Hospitality degree from a college in Glenwood Springs and went right to work at a small inn in Boulder," Jamie says. "About six months later, I lost that job when the owners decided to retire. I got a new job at a hotel in Denver, but less than a year after that they laid off a big chunk of the staff after a particularly slow convention season, myself included. After that, I was hired by a convention center, but it wasn't a good experience. Between having three jobs in two years and really not liking one of them, I began to think maybe hospitality wasn't as good a fit for me as I thought. I started to give serious thought to other career options."

What led Jamie to pursue a new career in health care was a memory from her childhood. "My brother came down with pneumonia when I was little," she says. "I remember visiting him in the hospital and seeing what good care the nurses were taking of him and how nice they were. I was absolutely wowed and thought nursing had to be the most amazing job in the world. That feeling came back to me when I started looking for other career opportunities." Her parents helped her stay motivated as well, especially when Jamie was nervous about having to go back to school. "My dad was big on us getting as much education as possible because he never finished his own degree. And when my brother and I were kids, both my parents would ask us questions like, 'What do you want to do when you grow up,' and then ask the heavier questions like, 'Think you'll have health benefits? Pension? What kind of salary do you think you'll make? Where can you go to school for that?' Maybe everyone's parents did that. So when I was thinking about making a switch, even before I settled on nursing, I was thinking of areas that would afford a decent pay and benefits."

Jamie needed to take a few prerequisite classes before she could enter nursing school, including a chemistry class. "That one was hard for

me. I hated chemistry class in high school and did terribly at it then, but this time was different. This time I applied myself because I was actually interested in it as a stepping stone toward what I wanted to do with my life." Once she got into a nursing program, she found those classes more enjoyable because they were less theoretical and more hands-on. "I learned better with those classes because first you learn about, let's say, chest pain and ways to treat it, then you see and do with a patient, and it just all connected in my brain." Not that she found it all a breeze. "One of the hardest things to learn was all the medical abbreviations for Greek, Latin, and medicine names."

One of her initial concerns about going back to school had to do with how she would pay for it, but she discovered there was help available. "I was able to get some financial assistance. I received two loans, one of which was from Sallie Mae. Both loans were for the nursing program, both low interest, and I didn't have to start paying them back until three to six months out of school. I paid one off in full in five years, and the other in eight. I also got a full TAP [Tuition Assistance Program] award from the state for three years of tuition." She went to school full-time but kept her position at the convention center as a part-time job. "I still wasn't happy there, but I needed the money and didn't have time to look for another job. I got through it by telling myself, 'It's only for a little longer, just one more year, six more months, one more month. . . .'"

Jamie reports that she did not have much difficulty finding work as a nurse after graduation. "I graduated in June that year and I think I had my first job by July, in a nursing home. I started my first hospital job the next January. Finding jobs wasn't that hard. I went to several area nursing homes and filled out applications, then to the three area hospitals and filled out applications. And I kept an eye on the paper. There always seemed to be nursing positions opening up. Thinking about it now, it's hard to believe I've been at my current hospital for almost 10 years, but I love it. It has its frustrations, and sometimes it can be downright heartbreaking, but I wouldn't trade it for the world. I feel like I found my calling."

Playing a positive role in her patients' lives is the number one aspect of being a nurse that Jamie loves about the job. "There are days when you wonder why you chose a job that involves so many bodily fluids, especially when you're emptying bedpans, but then you have moments where you make a real difference in someone's life and you realize it's completely worth it. Another thing I love is the camaraderie. Your coworkers become extended family. I spend half my holidays with my coworkers. Get a bunch of nurses in a room, serve a drink or two, and watch out! We can be very funny. We'll talk about the grossest stuff while eating—so a strong stomach is also key for the job. The people I work with now in the pain management unit at the hospital are wonderful. Some days we are so busy I never see the other nurses, but it is still a tight-knit group. I was just recently invited to the wedding of a nurse I mentored about five years ago." Jamie's hospital is a teaching facility, so she finds new knowledge abundant there. "I love to learn this way, hands-on. And I get to teach nursing students rotating through the unit. I've taught residents and new nurses to the floor."

Jamie doesn't just feel satisfied with her nursing job; she feels secure despite the recession. "Working in a state hospital, I wasn't too worried about losing my job, although I think we all get a little queasy when they talk budget cuts. So far no one has been let go, but they may not fill an empty slot right now. I don't know what it's like at the moment in private hospitals, but I think I'd be more nervous if I worked there."

For workers thinking about switching career paths to become nurses, Jamie advises not to do it just for the steady paycheck. "You need to really care about people and want to help, educate, teach, and care for them. One important trait to have is the ability to multitask—it's kind of like being a waitress on steroids. Having a huge bladder helps!" So does having good people and communication skills. "Remember that you're going to be dealing with the public a lot. My experience in hospitality prepared me for this, but if you've never dealt with the general public before, it can be a bit of a shock to learn how, let's say, challenging people can be, especially when they're in an extreme situation like

being in the hospital. You can't choose who your patients are. If you become a nurse, or anything else in health services, you're committed to helping people no matter what. I've been spat at by patients and called all sorts of nasty names; we even had to put a man in restraints once because he was so violent. But you soldier on and do your job. Patients and families are always asking questions—and this is another *very* important thing in nursing—if you don't know the answer to a question patients or family ask, say, 'I don't know the answer, but I'll find out.' People respect it when you tell the truth and then take the time to find out the answer. Lastly, I would make sure that people know that they're going to be dealing with death a lot. It's inevitable. You're going to have patients die and will have to deal with their grieving families. I suppose it takes a certain kind of person to be able to handle that. Being a nurse is physically, emotionally, and spiritually draining when it's what you love. And you have to love it."

CHAPTER 2

BIOTECHNOLOGY

Biotechnology, or biotech for short, may sound like something out of science fiction, but it has actually been around for millennia, ever since the earliest civilizations crossbred their domestic animals and genetically engineered their crops. Biotech refers to any technology that uses biological systems, organisms, and their derivatives to make or modify products, and the modern biotech field has applications in everything from food science to genetic research. However, today's biotech industry is primarily concerned with the manufacturing of medicine and pharmaceutical drugs.

In the previous chapter on health care, we discussed our aging population's escalating health needs driving that sector of industry into unprecedented growth. As those needs continue to grow, the creation of new drugs is one of the factors driving the health-care boom, and the result is that the biotech industry has seen the largest number of new venture-capital investments in recent years. As a necessary and cutting-edge development field, biotech is also one of the industries that has the been specifically targeted for the Obama administration's Recovery Act stimulus funding on both the state and federal level, including tax credits, grants, and loan programs that will ensure the industry's vitality and create thousands of new jobs. Increased growth is also expected with the Obama

administration lifting the restrictions on embryonic stem cell research, as well as the U.S. Food and Drug Administration's (FDA's) approval of clinical trials for drugs based on stem cell research.

Since the FDA approved the very first biotech drug in 1982, the industry has had nearly 300 more drugs approved, with another 300 currently in clinical development targeting more than 200 diseases. The good news is that the biotech field was only mildly affected by the recession. Big companies with strong balance sheets and low cash-burn rates are weathering the current turmoil and still generating revenue from product sales, though smaller companies in the development stage were hit by decreases in venture capital and mutual fund investments. However, with the Tufts Center for the Study of Drug Development reporting that traditional, multinational pharmaceutical companies are increasingly forming partnerships with newer biotech companies in order to boost new product development, and with major biotech firms increasingly outsourcing research and development operations to the smaller firms in order to meet revenue targets, the industry is expected to remain stable. In fact, biotech growth is expected to exceed that of the traditional pharmaceutical industry significantly over the next five years. In 2009, for example, 83 percent of pharmaceutical sales were from small-molecule or chemical products, which are the materials used by traditional pharmaceutical companies, and 15 percent from biologicals, the materials used by biotech. In 2010, 76 percent of sales are forecasted from small molecules and 22 percent from biologicals—though I've seen some estimates that say biologicals might provide as much as 60 percent of revenue. Estimates for the global biotech industry is forecast in 2010 to be worth over $100 billion, a 70 percent increase over its value in 2005. As the field's growth continues, so will the need for workers of diverse professional backgrounds.

The industry currently employs more than 200,000 people, with that number expected to increase 24 percent by 2016, ranking it among the fastest-growing American industries, due to the demand for their products remaining so strong. Even during fluctuating economic conditions, there will always be a market for over-the-counter and prescription drugs, including the diagnostics used in hospitals, laboratories, and homes; the vaccines routinely administered to infants and children; analgesics and other symptom-easing drugs; antibiotics and other drugs for life-threatening diseases; and popular "lifestyle" drugs such as Botox and Viagra for the treatment of non-life-threatening conditions.

Contrary to the image many people have of an industry wholly composed of scientists in white lab coats, only an approximate 28 percent of biotech jobs are actually in the professional science occupation. These include the following:

- Chemists, composing 5.2 percent of workers
- Medical scientists, compose 3.4 percent
- Computer specialists, composing 3.2 percent
- Biological technicians, composing 2.5 percent
- Chemical technicians, composing 2.3 percent
- Biochemists and biophysicists, composing 1.4 percent
- Engineering technicians, composing 1.2 percent
- Microbiologists, composing 1.1 percent
- Biomedical engineers, composing 0.8 percent
- Industrial engineers, composing 0.8 percent

On the other hand, approximately 16 percent of jobs in the field are in management, business, and financial occupations. These include the following:

- Top executives, composing 1.9 percent of workers
- Industrial production managers, composing 1.3 percent

- General business and project managers, composing
  1.3 percent
- Natural sciences managers, composing 1.1 percent
- Accountants and auditors, composing 1.1 percent
- Marketing and sales managers, composing 0.9 percent

Approximately 13 percent of biotech jobs are in office and administrative support occupations. These include the following:

- Secretaries and administrative assistants, composing
  3.1 percent of workers
- Shipping, receiving, and traffic clerks, composing
  1.4 percent
- Customer service representatives, composing 1.3 percent
- General office clerks, composing 1.2 percent
- Production, planning, and expediting clerks, composing
  1.1 percent
- Bookkeeping, accounting, and auditing clerks, composing
  0.9 percent

Additionally, about 3 percent of jobs in the field are in sales, mainly sales representatives.

For an industry with such a high-tech name, it may come as a surprise that the remaining 40 percent of roles in the biotech industry are in manufacturing, machine maintenance and repair, as well as transportation occupations that offer opportunities for both low-skilled and high-skilled workers. These include the following:

- Packaging and filling machine operators and tenders, who compose the highest amount of works in the industry at
  7 percent

- Mixing and blending machine setters, operators, and tenders, composing 3.6 percent
- Chemical equipment operators and tenders, composing 3.5 percent
- Inspectors, testers, sorters, samplers, and weighers, composing 3 percent
- Supervisors/managers of production and operating workers, composing 2.6 percent
- General maintenance and repair workers, composing 2.1 percent
- Separating, filtering, clarifying, precipitating, and still machine setters, operators, and tenders, composing 1.9 percent
- Team assemblers, composing 1.7 percent
- Laborers and freight, stock, and material movers, composing 1.6 percent
- Machine feeders and offbearers, composing 1.4 percent
- Packers and packagers, composing 1.4 percent
- Industrial machinery mechanics, composing 1.1 percent
- Chemical plant and system operators, composing 0.8 percent
- Extruding, forming, pressing, and compacting machine setters, operators, and tenders, composing 0.8 percent

The ongoing research and manufacture of new products to combat currently uncured diseases such as cancer, Alzheimer's, and heart disease continues to contribute to biotech employment growth. Demand will also increase as the population expands, because so many drugs are related to preventive or routine health care, rather than simply curing illnesses. The growing number of older Americans who require more health-care services will further stimulate demand, as will the rising health consciousness and expectations of the

general public and the growth of both public and private health insurance programs, which increasingly cover the cost of drugs and medicines. These factors, combined with continuing improvements in manufacturing processes, are all resulting in rapid employment growth.

The projected growth numbers in this industry are truly impressive. The percentage of growth for just about every role mentioned is a double-digit percentage, ranging from the mid-teens to the fifties. For instance, by 2016, the number of marketing and sales managers is expected to grow by 26 percent, the number of accountants and auditors also by 26 percent, computer specialists by 35.5 percent, industrial machinery mechanics by 44.9 percent, and industrial engineers by a whopping 53.1 percent.

Because biotech is different from most other manufacturing industries, it's not highly sensitive to changes in economic conditions. Even during periods of high unemployment, work in the biotech industry tends to remain relatively stable, and additional openings are constantly arising from the need to replace workers who transfer to other industries, retire, or leave the workforce for other reasons. The primary driver behind the industry's job growth is its maturation, supported by a strong product pipeline. After three decades of research, development, and production, biotechnology has come of age, especially with its monoclonal antibody products poised to see the greatest revenue growth.

Broad scientific advances and commercial successes have captured the attention and aspirations of policy makers, businesspeople, and investors alike in spurring biotech growth, but perhaps the most important driving market factor is the lack of generic drug competition. Traditional small-molecule drugs face a tremendous threat from generic competition, but the development of biologics provides protection for biotech

companies. This is fueling an increase in positions such as vaccine researchers and scientists with therapeutic protein experience. It is also ratcheting demand for researchers with biology degrees, representing quite a market shift for those workers. In the past, it was common to see individuals with biology degrees working as analytical chemists, but now, with the growth of the biotech industry, more bio grads are finding job opportunities in this field.

Innovation demands high investment in research and development, and as a result, biostatisticians and clinical research associates are the nation's first and third most in-demand jobs in the tech sector, respectively, according to the Yoh Index of Technology Wages. Other jobs in great demand include regional monitors, analytical and quality control chemists, clinical lab scientists, drug safety associates, protein purification and cell culture scientists, clinical data managers, and clinical project managers. Even manufacturing jobs are in demand because of the big push for the development of biologicals, though manufacturing a biological product is more complex than traditional small-molecule drugs, so skilled labor is critical to the production of these products.

Still, as you saw in the roles detailed above, biotech jobs are not all "lab coat required." A study in the *Journal of Commercial Biotechnology* found that bigger companies with products on the market had an average of 17 percent of job openings in the laboratory category and 83 percent of openings in the remaining non-laboratory categories, while smaller, start-up companies without products on the market had a higher percentage of jobs categorized as laboratory work. In other words, strong opportunities exist in the bigger biotech companies, which are also the most stable, for people with diverse backgrounds and skill sets, including computer specialists, such as systems analysts, biostatisticians, and computer support technicians, since

disciplines such as biology, chemistry, and electronics are continuing to converge and become more interdisciplinary, creating demand in rapidly emerging fields such as bioinformatics (a branch of biotech that uses information technologies to work with biological data like DNA) and nanotechnology (the science of engineering at a molecular level). Other positions include office workers with backgrounds ranging from secretary to accountant to executive, sales and marketing professionals, customer service representatives, and workers with traditional manufacturing, production, and shipping backgrounds.

To succeed and grow in the twenty-first-century economy, biotech employers are looking to fill each position in their companies, from entry-level to the most advanced, with qualified and skilled individuals. Because the industry is experiencing such rapid growth, biotech firms have a demand for more skilled workers than are available and are projected to need more workers than are currently enrolled in training programs. This discrepancy between workers availability and worker demand has led the Department of Labor to announce a series of investments in local schools and local/regional workforce investment systems totaling nearly $34 million to address the needs of the biotech industry. These investments include 16 High Growth Job Training Initiative grants totaling almost $23 million, and three Community-Based Job Training Grants totaling just over $11 million, which are designed to improve the role of community colleges in providing affordable, flexible, and accessible education for the nation's workforce. Leveraged resources from grantees total almost $24 million. These investments aren't just for expanding the pipeline of new graduates entering the biotech industry; they also exist to help workers from declining industries transition into biotech by building on their existing skills and training them for new ones.

State governments are getting in on biotech investments too, bringing new jobs and money to places that were hit hard by devastating losses in the manufacturing industry. North Carolina is an excellent example of this. The state has invested more than $1.2 billion in biotech in the past 10 years, between facilities, research, training programs, and incentives for companies. As a result, North Carolina now has more than 54,000 people working for some 500 biotech companies and is considered the third-largest biotech center in the nation, after California and Massachusetts. The aggregate economic impact, according to one report, is almost $46 billion a year.

Ultimately, the biotech industry is poised for massive growth with an expanding need for new, qualified personnel. Because our nation's health needs are growing and are so dependent on the medicines and drugs the biotech industry develops and manufactures, all signs point to it being a thriving career opportunity that will not only weather the current economic crisis nicely but go on to grow at an impressive rate and attract the best talent. In the appendix, you'll find a comprehensive list of biotech career resources, including industry news and job sites, and information on how to apply for related grants, scholarships, and loans.

MAKING THE TRANSITION: BIOTECHNOLOGY

Harold T., 49, of San Francisco, California, didn't even know what biotechnology was before he landed the job of comptroller at a Bay Area biotech firm. "When I first saw the ad listing for a job at a biotech company, I had to Google the word to find out what it was. All I could imagine was Frankenstein-type stuff." Now that he has been employed by a biotech firm for three years, he's got a better grasp on

what the field is about. "Back in the day, we just called them 'drug companies.' The term 'biotechnology' was completely new to me, but now it makes perfect sense to me and I can't imagine calling it anything else. I guess you really can teach an old dog new tricks."

Harold studied financial management in school. "My father was a private accountant with a lot of local clients who were family members, friends, and neighbors. Growing up, I was fascinated with the idea of working with numbers and wanted to follow in his footsteps, but at the same time, I knew I didn't want to work on my own the way he did. I'm much more of a people person than he was. I wanted to be part of a team." He figures it was this immersive background in finance that drove him to succeed. "I actually was awarded pretty good scholarships for both undergrad and graduate studies because my GPA reflected how determined I was to be a part of the financial field. Those scholarships helped considerably with offsetting the expense of getting my degrees. My father may have worked with money, but that doesn't mean my family had a lot of it. So I'm very grateful that those scholarships allowed me to pursue my goals."

But even graduating at the top of his class couldn't get Harold the job he thought he wanted. "As soon as I had my master's degree, I started looking for a job in a financial or insurance company in Oregon, where I was living at the time. But this was in late 1987, and after the 'Black Monday' stock market collapse, all of the firms implemented hiring freezes. I wound up taking a job as comptroller of a large paper manufacturing and supply company." There, Harold oversaw the accounting, auditing, and budget departments, directing the preparation of financial reports, income statements, balance sheets, and analyses of future earnings and expenses. "I never expected it to happen, but it turned out I really enjoyed using my financial training in the manufacturing sector instead of within an organization solely devoted to finance."

"It was an old paper company that had been in business for about 75 years," Harold continues, "but unfortunately, it couldn't compete anymore against Staples and the other big paper suppliers. So after

working there for almost two decades, I suddenly found myself out of a job when the company shut down. I was absolutely terrified about what to do next." That was when he spotted the job listing for a comptroller position with a biotech firm.

Besides not knowing what biotechnology was, another part of the ad gave Harold pause—the job was in California, not Oregon. "I talked about it with my wife, and she told me to go ahead and apply for the job. Our daughter was away at college and we'd always talked about moving out of Oregon someday, so we decided this might be the perfect opportunity after all." Harold applied for and, to his surprise, was offered the job. "To tell you the truth, I didn't think I was qualified to move into another field. After 20 years, all I knew was the paper business. I thought I'd have to be retrained and have to relearn everything." Yet Harold's existing skill set translated perfectly to the biotech industry. "Being comptroller of a biotech company turned out to be pretty much the same work I'd been doing back in Oregon for the paper company. I didn't need new training at all. I just had to learn about the company's products, clientele, budget expectations, sales projections, that sort of thing. It was no different from what I would do at any new job. I also didn't have to take a pay cut, which was something I was worried about."

Over the past year, Harold has watched the unemployment numbers go up and witnessed the layoffs of both his brother and one of his closest friends from industries they had worked in for nearly 30 years, but he doesn't feel like his own job is in jeopardy. "My coworkers and I are worried about it, of course, just like everyone else. The number of available research grants and venture investments in our business has gone down since the recession started, but so far it hasn't affected my job security at all. There hasn't even been talk of cutting back hours or scaling down benefits, because even if funding is getting tighter, sales of the products we've got on the market are still strong. I think I'm very lucky to have entered the biotechnology field when I did. I'm happy with my work, I'm making a good living, and I feel like I have a secure position. What more can anyone ask for, especially in today's economy?"

For workers of all stripes looking to enter the biotech industry, Harold advises, "If you're into computers, engineering, or science, I can't think of a better field to join right now than biotechnology. Even though pharmaceuticals have been around for ages, biotech itself is a relatively new industry, and it's not too late to get in on the ground floor. Even if you're like me and not a scientist or computer specialist, I highly recommend it. Just don't make the same mistake I almost did and assume you can't take your skill set from one industry into another. On the outside, biotechnology couldn't look more different from the paper company I used to work for, but once inside I was very gratified to discover that they have many of the same staffing needs as most other companies."

"Oh, and one more thing," he adds. "If you see a promising job listing and don't recognize what the industry is, be sure to Google it instead of passing it over. You never know where life's going to take you."

CHAPTER 3

EDUCATION

With about one in four Americans enrolled in educational institutions, education is the nation's second largest industry after health care, accounting for some 13.3 million jobs. Yet an April 2009 report by the National Commission on Teaching and America's Future states that more than half of the nation's teachers, baby boomers ages 50 and over, will be eligible for retirement in the next decade. This will inevitably lead to a "brain drain" in the education field that, over the next five or six years, will result in the loss of a third of the nation's teachers. Exacerbating the problem are low retention rates for young teachers. The Commission concludes that a sufficient number of teachers are recruited at colleges and universities, but many leave the field within five years. It's like trying to pour water into a glass with no bottom—there just aren't enough teachers to meet the demand.

Strangely enough, the current economic recession is actually the silver lining to this dilemma. The retirement of higher-paid teaching veterans will help save newer teachers' jobs, and because local governments know that protecting education has a lot of political support, Recovery Act money is expected to be used to create teacher training programs so that the demand for candidates no longer outstrips the supply.

With an increasing number of people out of work and unable to find new jobs in their preferred fields, schools are filling up with workers looking to get their feet in the door of other, more promising industries, resulting in an adult interest in degree programs, certifications, and additional training that has never been greater. As high schools and universities expand to meet this demand, and as more students wait out the recession in college and graduate programs, the need for teachers, administrators, assistants, and other staff will grow commensurately.

According to the Bureau of Labor Statistics, in January 2009 education was one of a very small handful of industries that saw job growth, adding between 33,000 and 38,000 jobs, while most every other industry suffered layoffs. In February 2009, the unemployment rate for educational services dropped to 4 percent from 5.3 percent in December 2008. That's 4.1 percentage points less than the national unemployment rate at the time of 8.1 percent. January 2009 also saw 75,000 job openings in education, compared to 65,000 in January 2008. Additionally, there were 40,000 new hires between December 2008 and January 2009, up from 31,000 to 71,000, respectively.

Monster.com's Employment Index, which tracks online job advertising and analyzes hiring patterns, backs up the Bureau's findings with some of its own. They too found the number of jobs advertised for most industries in steep decline—except for education. Employers in the education and training sector are advertising job openings more than ever, mostly due to a personnel demand caused by unemployed workers seeking new training, according to Monster's analysis. The number of advertised positions in education grew by 32 Index points in December 2008 alone, the same month the job market was really starting to collapse. That's an increase of 33.3 percent over December 2007's numbers.

As you can see from both Monster.com's and the Bureau of Labor Statistic's findings, education is more than a stable employment industry; it's a growing one. And it's only going to keep growing, with the Obama administration announcing in June 2009 that it's pledging $53 billion in Recovery Act funding to create 135,000 new education jobs, including teachers, principals, and support staff. By 2016, it's estimated that nearly 479,000 new jobs will be created.

With the demand for primary and secondary school teachers rising, especially in public schools and high-growth communities, some school districts are enticing candidates by offering tuition reimbursement and to pay recruits' student loans. The job security of being a teacher doesn't have to end at retirement either. Some districts rehire retired teachers as consultants or on a part-time basis, which is especially helpful in an economic climate where workers are seeing their retirement savings dwindle.

Opportunities in education run the gamut beyond just teachers and professors, but as you can see, teachers and other related education professionals do make up an impressive 67.4 percent of the field. These include the following:

- Postsecondary school teachers (i.e., those who teach at colleges and universities), who compose the largest number of employees in the entire industry at 12.4 percent of total workers
- Elementary school teachers, composing 11.4 percent
- Teachers' assistants, composing 8.3 percent
- Secondary school teachers, composing 7.8 percent
- Middle-school teachers, composing 4.9 percent
- Preschool through elementary-school special-education teachers, composing 1.6 percent
- Computer specialists, composing 1.5 percent

- Educational, vocational, and school counselors, composing 1.4 percent
- Kindergarten teachers, composing 1.2 percent
- Secondary-school special-education teachers, composing 1 percent
- Athletic team coaches and scouts, composing 0.9 percent
- Middle-school special-education teachers, composing 0.8 percent
- Self-enrichment education teachers (i.e., those who teach classes that students take for fun or self-improvement, such as cooking or knitting), composing 0.8 percent
- Secondary school vocational education teachers, composing 0.7 percent
- Registered nurses, composing 0.7 percent
- Librarians, composing 0.7 percent
- Instructional coordinators/curriculum specialists, composing 0.7 percent
- Preschool teachers, composing 0.5 percent
- Adult literacy, remedial education, and GED teachers and instructors, composing 0.5 percent
- Clinical, counseling, and school psychologists, composing 0.4 percent
- Speech-language pathologists/speech therapists, composing 0.4 percent
- Child, family, and school social workers, composing 0.3 percent

The next largest segment of the education industry, employing 11.3 percent of all workers, is office and administrative support. These include the following:

- Secretaries and administrative assistants, who compose 4.4 percent of all workers

- General office clerks, composing 2.8 percent
- Bookkeeping, accounting, and auditing clerks, composing 0.7 percent
- Library assistants, composing 0.3 percent

Next, an impressive 10.7 percent of the field is actually made up of service occupations. These include the following:

- Janitors and cleaners, who compose 3.6 percent of all workers
- Food service workers, composing 1.3 percent
- Cooks, composing 1.1 percent
- Child care workers (who care for children not yet old enough to enter school and supervise older children before and after school), composing 1 percent
- Security guards, composing 0.5 percent

Only 6.3 percent of workers in the education field are in management, business, and financial occupations, including elementary and secondary school administrators, such as principals, vice principals, and school superintendents, who compose 1.6 percent of the industry, and postsecondary school administrators, such as college presidents, who compose 1.0 percent

Lastly, 2.2 percent of all works are in the transportation occupation, such as school bus drivers, and 1.3 percent are in general maintenance and repair work, such as groundskeepers.

The overall education industry is expected to see an 11 percent growth by 2016, which doesn't look like a lot at first glance, but when you consider the fact that so many workers currently in the field are either approaching or have already reached retirement age, the overall demand for workers will increase substantially more than 11 percent. Also contributing

to growth is a mounting national emphasis on improving education and making it available not just to more children and young adults but also to those currently employed but in need of improving their skills, as well as an increasing number of students at each educational level as our nation's population continues to expand. The U.S. Department of Education recently released about $6 billion of its $44 billion Recovery Act spending plan to states like California, Illinois, and South Dakota to drive education reform, save jobs, and create new ones.

The continuing rise in enrollment for grades K to 12 is helping to generate demand for more workers in the education field as well. According to the National Center for Education Statistics, enrollment in public elementary and secondary schools rose an estimated 26 percent between 1985 and 2007. Public elementary school enrollment, which covers pre-kindergarten through 8th grade, is projected to increase by 10 percent between 2007 and 2016.

Educational reforms such as universal preschool and all-day kindergarten will require more preschool teachers (expected to grow 16 percent by 2016) and kindergarten teachers (expected to grow 15.9 percent). Also expected to grow at an accelerated rate is the number of special-education teachers in both primary school (expected to grow 18.9 percent) and middle school (expected to grow 16 percent), due to continued emphasis on the inclusion of disabled students in general-education classrooms and an effort to reach students with problems at younger ages. Similarly, school reforms that call for increased individual attention to students will require additional teachers' assistants, particularly to work with special-education and English-as-a-second-language students, pushing their number up an additional 6.5 percent by 2016.

Even in this difficult economy, parents are scrimping, saving, and sacrificing in their determination to provide their children with the education they need. With postsecondary education enrollment expected to grow at a faster rate as more high school graduates attend college, and as more working adults return to school to enhance or update their skills, employment of postsecondary teachers is projected to experience massive growth, from over 1.6 million in 2006 to 2 million in 2016—an impressive 23 percent increase.

Of course, there are opportunities within the halls of learning for non-teachers as well, as institutions continue to hire workers with diverse backgrounds in management, accounting, communications, law, information technology, administrative services, health care, transportation, janitorial, and food services. The number of child care workers employed by the education industry, for example, is expected to grow by 17.6 percent, while the number of bookkeepers and accountants is expected to grow by 9.9 percent.

Other roles in educational services that are expected to see excellent job opportunities include the following:

- Education administrators for preschool and child care centers and programs held 56,000 jobs in 2006 and are projected to reach 69,000 by 2016—a 24 percent increase.
- Self-enrichment teachers held 261,000 jobs in 2006 and are projected to reach 322,000 by 2016—a 23 percent increase.
- Coaches held 217,000 jobs in 2006 and are projected to reach 249,000 by 2016—a 15 percent increase.
- Adult literacy, remedial education, and GED teachers and instructors held some 76,000 jobs in 2006 and are projected to reach 87,000 by 2016—a 14 percent increase.

- Janitors and cleaners held over 2.3 million jobs in 2006 and are projected to reach over 2.7 million by 2016—a 14 percent increase.
- School counselors held 260,000 jobs in 2006 and are projected to reach 292,00 by 2016—a 13 percent increase.
- Cafeteria cooks held 401,000 jobs in 2006 and are projected to reach 445,000 by 2016—an 11 percent increase.
- School bus drivers held 455,000 jobs in 2006 and are projected to reach 497,000 by 2016—a 9 percent increase.

Many school districts, particularly in urban and rural areas, are having difficulty recruiting qualified teachers, administrators, and support personnel. Fast-growing areas of the country like the South and West are also having trouble recruiting education workers, especially teachers. Since the retirement rate will remain high through 2016, the number of new teachers entering the field probably won't be enough to meet the growing demand, and that should result in excellent job opportunities for candidates. Currently, alternative licensing programs are attracting more candidates, especially those from other career paths, but opportunities will continue to abound for highly qualified teachers, especially in those subject areas with the highest needs. The skills shortages in teaching have traditionally centered around math and science but are now including other subjects that reflect the changing, more technologically oriented world we live in, such as design, technology, communication, and information. In the appendix, you'll find a comprehensive list of education career resources, including certification courses, industry news, and job sites, and information on how to apply for related grants, scholarships, and loans.

MAKING THE TRANSITION: EDUCATION

Alex K., 43, is employed as a special-education teacher in his hometown of Queens, New York, but that position only came about after a long line of odd jobs. "I worked as a bookkeeper, video store clerk, camp counselor, and local reporter," he says. While he was deciding which career route he wanted to take, his aunt, who was the principal of a special-education school at the time, offered him a job as a teacher's aide. "Originally, I took the job to have something to do while I figured out what I wanted to do with my life," he explains. "That was almost 24 years ago."

Clearly, the job turned out to be a perfect fit. After nine years as an aide, Alex decided to capitalize on his natural proclivity for teaching and go back to school to earn the appropriate degrees necessary to become a full-fledged teacher. "I needed both a bachelor's degree and a master's degree," he says. "The bachelor's degree was in my chosen field, History, and the master's was in Special Education." In order to keep working at the school, Alex scheduled classes around his workday. "I started out going to classes at night and then went back to school full-time for my bachelor's. The master's was nights and summer classes."

When it came to paying for his certification, Alex considers himself among the fortunate. "I'm very lucky in that my school offers tuition reimbursement, and the city/state offers free graduate classes through the Department of Education. The classes are easy enough to come by, the Department of Education prints a course catalog every semester." The curriculum for his chosen field, however, was not an easy find. "The program I needed, teaching history to students with disabilities grade 9 to 12, is as rare as an eclipse. You'd think if the state required it, at least all the state university schools would offer it. You'd be wrong," he quips.

After finding the necessary program that suited his needs and schedule, Alex discovered his on-the-job training made passing his courses a breeze. After graduating, he decided to stay at the same special-education school he started at all those years ago rather than putting his skills

on the market, despite the fact that he is now part of a field that is in high demand. "With my special-education background, I would definitely have a leg up on the competition. With all the budget cuts, school districts are looking for ways to save money. One of the ways they do this is to limit the amount of students they send to schools like mine. A teacher with my background would be in high demand in a mainstream school district looking to keep their special ed students in the district."

Even with the recession, budget cutbacks, and short-term hiring freezes at some schools, he maintains that the, opportunities are still out there for teachers, especially in underserved areas. "It's easy to find a job in teaching if you're willing to go into more challenging schools and neighborhoods," Alex explains. "Many cities will offer attractive deals for new teachers. Las Vegas, for example, helps new teachers buy homes. Those homes, however, are often not where someone would necessarily prefer to live." Other employment opportunities are starting to appear in the education industry as well. "Recruitment is something new in education. Our science teacher was recruited through an education headhunter, but that's still a new field and science teachers are in big demand. Recruitment is probably bigger for administration jobs right now."

Still, even when it comes to teaching in what might be a less desirable district, Alex feels the trade-off is worth it. "I find my job very fulfilling. No one goes into teaching for the money, but you can't put a dollar value on not dreading work when I wake up in the morning." At the private special-education school where he teaches, Alex is an "employee-at-will," meaning his contract is for one year at a time. Even so, the recession never made him feel like his job was in danger of being lost. "Things have remained pretty stable," he reports.

Alex has quite a lot of down-to-earth advice to share with workers looking to transition into the education field, especially in the role of teacher. "If you think teaching is easy because we get all that vacation time, you'll burn out quickly," he says. "If you think teaching is like what you see on TV, you'll be in for quite a surprise. One of the things I used to love about the show *Boston Public* was that I could watch and play

'count the number of times I'd be fired' in each episode." Alex recommends a healthy dose of self-reliance and the ability to think on your feet as important ingredients for being a good teacher. "If teaching were just you and the kids, it would be spectacular. But there can be a lot of bureaucracy too. Be ready for a lot of frustration and varying degrees of help from parents and administrators. In fact, the skill set I've found most difficult to learn is navigating the educational bureaucracy. If you find someone who has mastered this, please put me in touch with them."

He also advises prospective educators to get rid of their rose-colored glasses right away so that they can take the job seriously and approach it with their eyes open, especially to the fact that every job, no matter how noble, has its frustrations. "Always remember, just because a person goes into teaching or education doesn't make them a saint. You get the same petty personality clashes and junior high school-type cliques in education as you do anywhere else." Just as important, he says, is entering the field prepared with the knowledge that the first schools teachers are hired by are rarely their dream schools. "Most new teachers get placed in struggling schools in underserved neighborhoods thanks to union rules on seniority." He adds with his wry sense of humor, "Teaching is the absolute worst best job you'll ever have."

CHAPTER 4

GREEN ENERGY

We all remember the summer of 2008, when the average price for regular gasoline in the United States hit a record high of $4.11 a gallon, going even higher in some areas, such as parts of Michigan, where gas hit a jaw-dropping $5.09 per gallon. It was brutal, especially when coupled with the news that oil companies were posting record quarterly profits at the same time, which led to a national, populist backlash against the industry. Still, something very interesting and beneficial came out of 2008's gas crisis, namely, a new and lasting national interest in alternative and renewable sources of energy, called "green energy," as well as in the environment as a whole.

Before we get into green energy, let's take a moment to see how the traditional energy industry is faring by way of comparison.

While I wouldn't go so far as to say the traditional energy companies are stagnating, we are seeing hiring freezes, projects being eliminated, and a number of related signals that indicate many energy companies are following the rest of the economy into a standstill. The projected employment numbers for most of the energy industry by the year 2016 aren't promising. In the utilities sector, electric power generation, transmission, and distribution is forecasted to see a 5.3 percent

decrease in employment, while natural gas is projected to see a 17.6 percent *decrease*. To be fair, it's not all gloom and doom. There is *some* job growth to be found in utilities, mainly because almost half of gas and electric workers will reach retirement age by 2016. Utilities companies are doing what they can to replace retiring workers, but the variety of careers available to people with technical skills is making it difficult to find enough applicants to fill these openings. In fact, as you can see in the following list, the only areas of projected growth for gas and electric reflect this need for highly skilled professionals and production personnel:

- Nuclear power reactor operators, who compose 0.6 percent of the industry, are expected to grow by 10.3 percent.
- Industrial engineers, who compose 0.4 percent, are expected to grow by 7.2 percent.
- Industrial machinery mechanics, who compose 1.4 percent, are expected to grow by 6.9 percent.
- Power plant operators, who compose 4.4 percent, are expected to grow by 0.9 percent.
- Nuclear technicians, who compose 0.6 percent, are expected to grow by 0.8 percent.
- Electrical engineers, who compose 2.3 percent, are expected to grow by 0.5 percent.
- Electrical power line installers and repairers, who compose 10.4 percent, are expected to grow by 0.4 percent.
- Nuclear engineers, who compose 0.8 percent, are expected to grow by 0.2 percent.

So the numbers aren't that promising, especially when you consider that's only eight roles for a sector composed of hundreds. However, some good news was just recently announced that could turn around those dismal job growth numbers for

the natural gas industry. In July 2009, the U.S. Senate unveiled a bill that would encourage the development of natural gas engines and infrastructure, and increase the tax credits that buyers would receive for purchasing vehicles that run on natural gas, boosting it from $5,000 to $12,500. The bill also includes a provision to deploy more filling stations for natural-gas-powered vehicles. Still, it's unknown how much of an effect this will have on manufacturing or the natural gas sector. Currently, only one car is offered to American drivers that run on compressed natural gas (CNG)—the Honda Civic GX—but there have been less than 2,000 sold and there still aren't a whole lot of places to fill them up on the road. In total, there are about 142,000 CNG vehicles in the United States, the great majority of which are public transportation buses, and even then, only 20 percent of all buses run on CNG. When it comes to possible job growth in the natural gas sector, it's best to take a "wait and see" approach for now.

Things do look slightly better for the oil and coal industries, especially with the widespread global discussions happening now about "clean coal"—in particular, the variety of carbon capture and storage (CCS) technologies currently being researched that could mitigate the environmentally harmful effects from fossil fuel power plants. About half of U.S. power comes from coal, and the process of burning coal for electricity accounts for about 80 percent of the country's CO_2 emissions from the energy industry, according to the Energy Information Administration. With coal likely to remain one of the nation's lowest-cost electric power sources for the foreseeable future, given our enormous reserves, the Obama administration has pledged a commitment to advance clean coal technologies. U.S. investment in CCS research, development, and deployment is expected to reach $7.2 billion by 2010. However, with the recession limiting available funds and the jury

still out on the viability of CCS technologies, clean coal might still be decades away. As a result, the energy industry isn't seeing substantial growth from the clean coal news just yet.

Oil and coal aren't going away anytime soon, but the extraction sector as a whole is projected to experience a 1.6 percent *decrease* in employment by 2016, mainly because of new technologies and new extraction techniques that increase productivity while requiring fewer workers. Still, the growth of some individual occupations in oil and coal show more promising numbers than in the utilities sector, though once again, we see only a pressing need for workers with specific, related skills. The occupations are as follows:

- Quarry rock splitters, who compose 0.5 percent of the industry, are expected to grow by a whopping 28.3 percent.
- Mobile heavy-equipment mechanics, who compose 1.6 percent, are expected to grow by 8.2 percent.
- Industrial machinery installation, repair, and maintenance workers, who compose 4.2 percent, are expected to grow by 6.5 percent.
- Welding, soldering, and brazing workers, who compose 1 percent, are expected to grow by 5.2 percent.
- Separating, filtering, clarifying, precipitating, and still machine setters, operators, and tenders, who compose 0.5 percent, are expected to grow by 4.7 percent.
- Geoscientists, who study the composition, structure, and physical aspects of the Earth, who compose 1.3 percent, are expected to grow by 4.5 percent.
- Electricians, who compose 1.4 percent, are expected to grow by 4.2 percent.
- Engineers, who compose 3.4 percent, are expected to grow by 4 percent.

- Continuous mining machine operators, who compose 1.5 percent, are expected to grow by 3.8 percent.
- Evacuating and loading machine and dragline operators, who compose 2.2 percent, are expected to grow by 3.6 percent.
- Mine cutting machine operators, who compose 1.2 percent, are expected to grow by 3.5 percent.
- Geological and petroleum technicians, who compose 1.1 percent, are expected to grow by 3 percent.
- Construction equipment operators, who compose 4.6 percent, are expected to grow by 2.8 percent.
- Computer specialists, who compose 1.3 percent, are expected to grow by 2.8 percent.
- Truck drivers, who compose 4.5 percent, are expected to grow by 1.5 percent.
- Mining roof bolters, who compose 0.7 percent, are expected to grow by 1.2 percent.
- Business and financial operations occupations, such as compliance officers, accountants, and budget analysts, who compose 4 percent, are expected to grow by 1 percent.

The challenging news for the oil refining industry is that it faces tougher times ahead as higher operating costs and falling demand for petroleum products weigh on the bottom line, likely forcing some plants to close. Consulting firm Deloitte estimates that refiners could cut production of up to 1.5 million barrels per day, or about 9 percent of the nation's current refining capacity, due to stricter fuel economy standards for cars, rising mandates for blending ethanol and other biofuels into the fuel supply, and pending climate change legislation that could cause refiners to add costs as they invest in technology to reduce greenhouse gas emissions at facilities. Coupled with the U.S. Energy Information Administration forecasting a 13 percent

reduction in gasoline demand between now and 2030, this can only result in fewer available jobs.

On the other side of the coin, however, we find exponential growth in the green energy sector. According to a report by the Environmental Industries Commission, this is already a $3 trillion global marketplace, which is growing rapidly at over 5 percent a year. Employment in green energy in the United States is expected to grow as much as 25 percent in the next decade, especially with President Obama's call for the creation of 5 million "green-collar" jobs that would employ workers with a wide variety of skill sets. While Americans are betting that manufacturing wind turbines, solar panels, and electric cars will put the country back on top of the manufacturing game, there's even better news attached to the green energy initiative. Namely, those 5 million new jobs would bring back *more than half* of all the manufacturing jobs lost in this country since the sector's heyday in the late 1970s. Even more optimistic is the nonprofit American Solar Energy Society, which is forecasting as many as 37 million jobs from renewable energy and energy efficiency by 2030—that's 17 percent of all U.S. employment.

The Green Collar Jobs Report from the American Solar Energy Society and Management Information Services, Inc., finds the renewable energy and energy efficiency industries as a whole represented more than 9 million jobs and over $1 billion in revenue in 2007, growing three times as fast as the U.S. economy. The Department of Labor's Bureau of Labor Statistics (BLS) does not currently have any numbers on the green energy job market, but part of President Obama's 2010 budget provides $8 million for the BLS to work with other Department of Labor agencies and key organizations, such as the Energy Information Administration, the Bureau of Economic Analysis, and the National Science Foundation, to define the green

economy and produce data on green-collar jobs. Those findings won't even be published until 2011, but in the meantime, the expected job numbers for each green energy subsector are promising:

- *Advanced biofuels.* The research, development, and manufacturing of these alternative, organic sources of fuel—including using plant material or animal waste to create hydrocarbons; converting sugarcane, corn, and switchgrass into ethanol and gasohol for combustion engines; and blending chemically processed plant oils with petroleum diesel fuel to make biodiesel—is expected to add 29,000 new jobs by 2012, and 190,000 new jobs by 2022. As a primarily venture-backed industry, biofuels are mostly insulated from the broader economy and will be seeing considerable job growth as awareness about global warming combines with the strong desire Americans have to keep their energy dollars inside the country instead of sending billions overseas. Some states are stepping in to make sure biofuels continue to be a robust source of energy and employment. For instance, Virginia passed a $4 million bioscience bill that provides tax credits, grants, and loans to help expand the industry, with more money on the way once the economy improves. North Carolina's backing of biofuels as an engine of economic growth, in conjunction with their Green Business Development Fund, has resulted in a flurry of tax incentives for companies, which will keep employment numbers high.
- *Energy-efficient infrastructure.* "Green buildings" help companies cut energy costs and build sound financial situations, and as a study by the Center for American Progress finds, such green investments on a wide scale

will ignite the economy of the nation as a whole. A $100 billion green infrastructure investment over 10 years, with a focus on green building retrofits and investment in alternative energy sources, could be entirely paid for with proceeds from carbon permit auctions under a greenhouse gas cap-and-trade program, if that program goes through. That's roughly the same amount of investment as the tax rebate checks sent as part of the April 2008 economic stimulus plan, but the program would actually create 300,000 more jobs. The design and construction of energy-efficient buildings, as well as retrofitting existing buildings to be more efficient, will put engineers, architects, and a deeply wounded construction industry back to work, even without cap-and-trade, with approximately 280,000 new jobs, nearly half of which are expected to be created in the first months of 2010 alone. Additionally, a study by the Apollo Alliance, a San Francisco-based coalition of labor, business, environmental, and community leaders, has recommended to the government an additional $89.9 billion investment in financing that could eventually create 827,260 jobs in green buildings. The truly great thing about the transition to an energy-efficient infrastructure is that well over 90 percent of the total spending involved will occur within the U.S. economy. Energy efficiency measures like building retrofits, public transportation improvements, and upgrading the electrical grid can only occur on-site. Weatherization projects for buildings in Michigan can only be done in Michigan. The New York City subway system can only be upgraded in New York.

- *Solar energy.* Solar panel technology has been around for decades—President Carter was already talking about it in the 1970s—and solar power companies currently employ

25,000 to 35,000 workers across approximately 3,400 companies, with the potential to grow by 110,000 new jobs by the end of 2010 if the anticipated tax credits are accelerated. New tax incentives from state and local governments are promoting expansion in this industry, increasing incentives for homeowners to install solar panels on their roofs. Although still a relatively small part of green energy production, growing solar energy demand is expected to create new jobs across the country.

- *Wind energy.* The design, manufacture, and installation of wind turbines is expected to create 185,000 new jobs by the end of 2010, and 500,000 new jobs by 2030. Wind is already the leading and fastest-growing source of alternative energy in the United States, employing some 85,000 workers and supplying about 1 percent of the nation's electricity, powering the equivalent of 4.5 million homes, with wind farms operating in 34 states across the country. A recent report by the U.S. Department of Energy suggests that wind power could eventually contribute 20 percent of the nation's electricity by 2030. Nine billion dollars was invested in 2007, driving a production increase of 21 percent, and in 2008 the United States became the world's leading provider of wind power. A recent study by Emerging Energy Research, a consulting firm in Cambridge, Massachusetts, projects an additional $65 billion in investments through 2015, which will lead to more job opportunities in the field.

Right now, wind energy seems poised to see the most near-term job growth. Positive support for wind energy is overwhelming, as evidenced by the record attendance at the 2009 WINDPOWER Conference, sponsored by the American Wind Energy Association (AWEA), where the number of exhibitors

and attendees were both up more than 50 percent from 2008. While our nation's wind energy industry began by importing turbines, equipment, and technology from Europe, there is now a steady growth opportunity in the United States for domestic equipment and component manufacturing, parts and supply, and contract construction, all of which point to attractive employment opportunities. For example, more than eight new wind turbine manufacturing plants were opened in the United States in 2008, with another 19 facilities announced. In total, during the 2007 to 2008 period there were 70 new wind energy facilities announced, added, or expanded in the United States, with 55 of them being manufacturing locations. It is estimated that about 50 percent of all components for U.S. wind turbine installations are now manufactured in the United States, with that share increasing steadily. Additionally, there is significant support and investment by European manufacturers in U.S. wind power, like the Danish firm Vesta, the world's leading wind turbine manufacturer, which recently opened a manufacturing facility in Brighton, Colorado, and is currently planning a factory in Pueblo, Colorado, that will employ some 400 workers—quite a boon to the manufacturing industry that was hit hard by the recession—with roles ranging from managers to engineers, machinists to technicians.

Developers of wind farms, where those turbines are put to use, are similar to real estate developers in that the economics of a facility must be attractive enough over time to warrant the investment, construction, and operation of the wind farm. Today's typical wind farms may have 100 to 300 wind turbines installed and could cost from $1.4 million to $3 million per turbine, a figure that includes all the land and infrastructure involved. A development team for such a facility would include roles like meteorologists, real estate/land procurement personnel, engineers, environmental permitting staff, financial analysts,

and wind technicians—all to determine feasibility, secure financing, and plan, engineer, and construct the facility, typically a four-year process. After that, once it's up and running, there are operations and maintenance requirements for the facility that will extend throughout the next 20 to 30 years, with employment opportunities for many of the same roles that are employed in traditional power generation facilities.

Similarly, employment opportunities will exist for those transitioning into the electric power generation sector, which also includes the electric power grid. As wind farm installations are added across the United States, it is creating the challenge of transporting electric power from areas with high wind resources, which are typically less populated, to high-demand areas, which typically have large populations. Additions will have to be made to the existing electric grid system, and that will spur employment as well, especially for planners, engineers, financial workers, construction workers, line maintenance workers, electrical contractors, and others. According to industry group GridWise Alliance, the creation of a new "smart grid" could generate some 280,000 new jobs. Even more, they estimate federal investment in a smart grid could lead to an unspecified, but substantially larger, number of indirect jobs as well, with the deployment of smart-grid technology enabling other types of green technology, including plug-in hybrid and electric vehicles, distributed renewable energy and wind energy generation.

Green energy was becoming a larger part of U.S. energy production even before the recent push. According to the Energy Information Administration, in 2006 about 7 percent of U.S. energy was produced by green energy, with the American Solar Energy Society reporting that there were about 106,000 jobs in green energy that same year. In 2007, the field grew by an additional 7 percent.

Massive investments, subsidies, and incentives from state and local governments are spurring the current growth, as is the federal Recovery Act, which includes billions of dollars for home energy-efficiency upgrades and the extension of a tax credit for renewable-energy technologies. Additionally, approximately $100 million in grant funds will be made available to provide training and placement services in green energy industries for workers impacted by national energy and environmental policy, individuals in need of updated training related to green energy industry, and unemployed workers, providing the training that will prepare workers to enter the green energy industry, as well as green occupations within other industries like construction and architecture. A portion of these funds will also be specifically geared toward communities impacted by the collapse of the automotive industry. Another $150 million in grant funds will be used to create training and placement services that provide pathways out of poverty and into green energy employment. Approximately $190 million in grant funds will be made available to State Workforce Investment Boards across the country to create strategies in tune with states' energy policies and local and regional training activities that lead to green energy employment, giving states an opportunity to develop a statewide energy strategy and fostering the development of a national workforce that's ready to meet the demands of the green energy industries. A portion of these funds will also be reserved for communities affected by the auto industry collapse. Approximately $5 million in grant funds will be earmarked for projects that expand Department of Labor-funded training programs to ensure that targeted groups are prepared to meet the needs of our country's expanding green energy industry, providing training for entry-level positions leading to career pathways and/or additional training for green jobs. As you can see, the government is backing green energy to the

hilt, fully aware that harnessing the power of clean, renewable energy will fuel our economy for decades to come.

Green energy production differs from state to state. Like traditional energy sources, green energy relies on the geography that supports it, but it also relies on investments, usually by state and local governments, which make renewable energy an affordable alternative for utility companies. Texas is a great example of this. The Lone Star State has invested heavily in wind energy and now has greater wind-energy capacity than any other state in the union, with 3 percent of its electricity coming from wind, enough to supply power to 1 million homes.

All this growth is great news for people who are interested in careers that help the environment. A study by the Renewable and Appropriate Energy Laboratory at the University of California in Berkeley finds that renewable energy creates more jobs per kilowatt hour than traditional energy sources. Granted, when the bills are due and the bank account is dwindling, the environment doesn't tend to top anyone's list of priorities, but the good news is that for those who have already started working in traditional energy occupations, many skills are transferable. Jobs in green energy are not that different from jobs in traditional energy, or construction, or any manufacturing industry, really. Imagine the economic impact of putting all those automakers and construction workers currently unemployed or underutilized because of the recession back to work, repurposing their existing skills to build and install wind turbines, solar energy panels, and electric car batteries, and you have an idea of what a key driver of economic stabilization and job growth green energy really is.

The jobs it will create stretch across every occupation, from manual labor to highly skilled specialists. Solar and wind turbine manufacturing plants will need assembly line workers. Mechanics, electricians, and maintenance workers will be needed for wind farms, solar parks, and biofuels plants.

A variety of science and engineering positions will be central to the growth of the industry, with an emphasis on mechanical and electrical engineering. Since about 65 percent of green jobs right now are with companies that recycle waste, cut greenhouse gas pollution, and handle water conservation, according to a study by the Pew Charitable Trusts released in June of 2009, many of the jobs require little or no additional training and transition smoothly to the green industry, such as accountants, stock clerks, security guards, and electricians. Because such immense growth is anticipated, community colleges around the country are already offering fast-track training courses for the more specialized jobs, such as solar panel installation, wind turbine repair, and biofuels processing.

All green energy companies will have a need for a variety of professionals with business backgrounds, including management, finance, law (especially environmental law), communications, information technology, sales, human resources, and administrative services. Other occupations like electricians, carpenters, plumbers, and laborers are called for as well. That's the real promise of the green industry—anyone, with almost any skill set, can tap into the growing green economy for a stable, long-lasting career.

In particularly high demand will be computer software developers and engineers, as the industry will need both occupations to design, build, and maintain the network of sensors and stochastic modeling that underpins wind farms, smart energy grids (which are also seeing massive government investment as part of the Recovery Act), and other green energy systems. Computer software developers are already forecasted to see a nearly 40 percent increase in employment by the year 2016, and industrial engineers by 20 percent. With the green boom that's about to hit, expect those percentages to increase even more.

A number of other specific occupations are expected to expand significantly as a result of the green energy industry's growth and the national interest in environmental issues. Although, once again, there is no standard definition of green-collar jobs or breakdown of the roles yet, the BLS has highlighted a number of related occupations associated with protecting and preserving the environment and natural resources. These include the following:

- Environmental engineers, of which there are about 54,000 in the United States, are expected to grow by 25 percent by 2016 as more are needed to comply with environmental regulations and to develop methods of cleaning up existing hazards. Demand will also grow due to a shift in emphasis from controlling existing problems to preventing future ones, as well as the increasing public health concerns resulting from population expansion. Because of this employment growth, job opportunities will continue to flourish even as more and more students earn degrees and enter the workforce. Federal, state, and local governments employ 21 percent of all environmental engineers, while 79 percent are employed by private companies, consulting firms, and universities.
- Environmental engineering technicians, of which there are just under 21,000 in the United States, are also expected to see 25 percent employment growth by 2016 as more workers are needed to apply the theories and principles of environmental engineering toward modifying and operating the equipment and devices used in pollution prevention and waste treatment. Federal, state, and local governments employ about 15 percent of environmental engineering technicians, while 85 percent are employed by private companies, consulting firms, and universities.

- Environmental scientists, of which there are over 80,000 in the United States, are also forecast to see 25 percent growth by 2016 as more workers are needed to conduct research into identifying and eliminating hazards that affect people, wildlife, air, food, water, and soil to determine the way to clean and preserve the environment during activities like waste disposal, land and water reclamation, construction, and other environmental changes. Federal, state, and local governments employ 43 percent of environmental scientists, while 57 percent are employed by private companies, consulting firms, and universities.
- Environmental science and protection technicians, of which there are 37,000 in the United States, are expected to see a 28 percent increase in employment by 2016 as more workers are needed to perform laboratory and field tests monitoring environmental resources and determining the contaminants and sources of pollution in the environment. Federal, state, and local governments employ about 30 percent of environmental science and protection technicians, while about 70 percent are employed by private companies, consulting firms, and universities.

Related Growth Industries

Two other promising high-growth offshoots of the green movement are actually green—as in plants.

Sustainable Forest Management

In March of 2009, the United Nations urged countries around the world to invest in green jobs that are working with sustainable forest management to address the growing problem

of worldwide unemployment, projecting that such an investment could create 10 million jobs. The United States took up
the challenge, making sustainable forest management a part of
the Recovery Act funding. Sustainable forest management
would involve managerial jobs such as monitoring and managing how much wood is taken out of a forest by logging to
ensure the forest doesn't become depleted and can grow back
fully. Managers would also make sure the wood harvest
wouldn't affect biodiversity and the water supply by working
in conjunction with environmental scientists and engineers.

Currently, there are only about 13,000 foresters in the United
States, and more than half of them work for federal, state, and
local governments, mostly in the Department of Agriculture's
Forest Service, the Department of the Interior's Bureau of Land
Management, and the Natural Resources Conservation Service.
A small number of foresters are self-employed, generally working as consultants or procurement foresters, while others work
for the logging and forestry industries. Their employment
numbers had only been expected to grow 5 percent by 2016,
but with a large number of workers set to retire over the next
decade, the number of job openings will be much bigger—and
will grow even more if the government's sustainable forest
management initiative comes through.

Organic Agriculture

The second impressive offshoot of the green industry is an
increase in organic agriculture, a worldwide growth industry
and a profitable, sustainable business that U.S. agricultural pro-
ducers are getting in on. The number of agricultural jobs on
traditional farms is expected to *decrease* by about 8 percent by
2016 because of a number of factors—chief among them, farms
being bought up by agri-conglomerates, the ability of an

increasingly mechanized industry to produce more with fewer workers, and the average age of the nation's roughly 2 million farmers being 55, just a decade away from retirement—but organic agriculture is set to fill the void. As an industry, organic agriculture uses small-scale, local, organic methods rather than petroleum-based machines and fertilizers, which means there will be a mounting need for more farmers to cultivate those fields, possibly up to tens of millions of farmers.

Organic agriculture has grown at a rate of about 20 percent per year for the last seven years, and industry experts are continuing to forecast additional growth. A study undertaken by the Organic Trade Association found that U.S. sales of organic food and beverages grew from a $1 billion industry in 1990 to an approximately $25 billion industry in 2008. In addition, the survey reported that organic sales in 2006 composed 2.8 percent of overall food and beverage sales, growing 20.9 percent in just that year alone. Adding to the viability of the industry is the fact that organically grown and produced ingredients are also used in such nonfood items as personal care products, apparel, textiles, toys, supplements, pet foods, and even some biofuels, with organic nonfood sales growing 26 percent in 2006. Global demand for organic products continues to grow, with sales increasing by over $5 billion a year, according to the World of Organic Agriculture: Statistics & Emerging Trends 2008 report, with the United States and the European Union making up 95 percent of the market.

Although the BLS doesn't have any numbers yet on the makeup of organic farms, for our purposes we can assume that because it's the method of production that sets organic agriculture apart from traditional farming, the roles will be basically the same.

As you might expect, 58.4 percent of all workers are in the farming, fishing, and forestry occupations. These include the following:

- Crop, nursery, and greenhouse farmworkers and laborers, who compose 40.4 percent of workers
- Ranch animal farmworkers, who compose 5.2 percent
- Agricultural equipment operators, who compose 3.9 percent
- Logging workers, who compose 3 percent
- Supervisors/workforce managers, who compose 2.2 percent
- Agricultural product graders and sorters, who compose 1 percent
- General agricultural workers, such as pickers, inspectors, and breeders, who compose 1 percent
- Fishers and related fish workers, who compose 0.9 percent
- Forest and conservation workers, who compose 0.6 percent

Management, business, and financial occupations make up 20.8 percent. These include the following:

- Farm, ranch, and other agricultural managers, who compose 18.7 percent of all workers
- Top executives, who compose 0.7 percent
- Accountants and auditors, who compose 0.6 percent

Transportation workers make up 5.6 percent of the industry. These include the following:

- Heavy truck drivers, who on traditional farms compose 1.8 percent of all workers, but on organic farms may compose less
- Laborers and material movers, who compose 1.8 percent
- Packers and packagers, who compose 1 percent
- Delivery service truck drivers, who on traditional farms compose 0.7 percent, but on organic farms may compose less

- Tractor and other industrial vehicle operators, who on traditional farms compose 0.6 percent, but on organic farms may compose less

Office and administrative support occupations make up 4.4 percent of the industry. These include the following:

- Bookkeeping, accounting, and auditing clerks, who compose 1.6 percent of all workers
- Secretaries, who compose 0.7 percent
- Material recording, scheduling, dispatching, and distributing occupations, such as couriers and dispatchers, who compose 0.5 percent
- Executive and administrative assistants, who compose 0.5 percent
- General office clerks, who compose 0.3 percent

Service occupations make up 4 percent of the industry. These include the following:

- Landscaping and groundskeeping workers, who compose 1 percent of all workers
- Animal trainers, who compose 0.9 percent
- Building cleaning workers, who compose 0.6 percent
- Security guards, who compose 0.4 percent
- Animal caretakers, who compose 0.4 percent

Production occupations make up 2.1 percent of the industry. These include the following:

- Food processing occupations, such as butchers and meat packers, who compose 0.5 percent of all workers
- Other production occupations, such as sorters, samplers, and weighers, who compose 0.9 percent

Professional and related occupations make up 1.7 percent of the industry. These include the following:

- Life scientists, who study animals, soil, and plants, compose 0.7 percent of all workers
- Agriculture and food science technicians, who on traditional farms compose 0.4 percent, but on organic farms may compose less

Installation, maintenance and repair occupations make up 1.3 percent of the industry. These include the following:

- Industrial machinery installation, maintenance, and repair workers, who on traditional farms compose 0.5 percent of all workers, but on organic farms may compose less
- Heavy vehicle and mobile equipment service technicians and mechanics, who on traditional farms compose 0.4 percent, but on organic farms may compose less

Construction jobs make up the last 1 percent of the industry. These include the following:

- Construction laborers, who compose 0.3 percent of workers
- Operating engineers/construction equipment operators, who compose 0.3 percent

One need look no further for proof of the greening of America than Walmart's plan, announced in July of 2009, to measure and inform customers of the sustainability of each product it sells. The giant retailer, which earned $406 billion in revenues in 2008, took about a year to develop this ambitious and comprehensive "sustainability index," and it will likely take another year or two for labels to start appearing on products on the shelf, allowing customers to make purchasing choices for themselves based on

environmental impact. One positive side effect of this plan will undoubtedly be more manufacturers of consumer products digging deep into their supply chains, measuring their environmental impact, including how much energy is consumed in manufacturing those products, and competing on terms of environmental sustainability for favorable treatment from the world's most powerful retailer—and that could mean more green-collar jobs added to the manufacturing sector in the near future.

With such amazing growth numbers, it's easy to see why green-collar jobs in everything from energy to construction to agriculture will be one of the prime sources of stable, lasting careers in the twenty-first century. Coupled with the massive development grants and funds being offered by federal, state, and local governments, the green industry is poised to not only provide millions of jobs but to energize the national economy as well. In the appendix, you'll find a comprehensive list of green career resources, including certification courses, industry news, and job sites, and information on how to apply for related grants, scholarships, and loans.

MAKING THE TRANSITION: GREEN ENERGY

Anna P., 41, of Dallas, Texas, has worked in manufacturing all her adult life but never imagined she'd find herself building 75-foot blades for a local clean energy company's wind turbines. "I got my first job right out of high school at a sheet metal factory," she says. "I was actually one of the first female workers on that company's production floor. I liked it so much that for the next 20 years, sheet metal was my life. Now I like to think I traded gray for green."

But together they hit the Internet and did some research. "We found out Texas is the second biggest state in America when it comes to clean energy companies, and the sixth biggest in the world for wind power. Neither of us knew that, but once we found out, I decided I was definitely on the right path and should go for it."

Anna took a proactive approach to finding a job in wind power. "I looked up all the local companies online and started sending off my résumé, either through their Web sites or through the mail, and I found some online job sites too. I started by applying to the ones that were the closest to where I live, since I was getting tired of dealing with traffic and long commutes." Eventually, she was referred to, and hired by, an independent manufacturing plant that has an exclusive contract with one of the city's largest wind power companies. "It wasn't the closest one to home, but the commute's not so bad," Anna admits. "I was hired just in time too. This was early December, and after that things really hit the fan." One month later, in January 2009, more than 200,000 workers throughout the country's manufacturing sector lost their jobs in a single month.

Anna, however, did not. "My job stayed put, and I'm grateful for that. I heard there were some layoffs at other clean energy companies, but not as bad as everywhere else, and not at my company." Though Anna took a slight pay cut when she accepted the job manufacturing the blades for wind turbines, she sees it as a worthwhile trade-off. "Less money is better than no money, and you can't really put a price on job security anyway. If I'd gone back to a sheet metal factory instead of coming here, there isn't a doubt in my mind that I would have lost that job right away with all the layoffs that are happening. Plus, clean energy is really picking up now, and it's kind of refreshing to be part of an industry that's on its way up instead of on its way down. I like that a lot."

But her job satisfaction isn't only about the sense of security she feels. "I also feel like I'm making a difference in my own small way," she says. "Maybe it sounds hokey, but I like to think that I'm making the

Anna worked for six different sheet metal companies over those two decades. "They were good jobs, but whenever the factories closed or downsized, I found myself having to look for a new job all over again. It was getting harder and harder each time. Partially because there were fewer companies hiring, and partially because I was getting older and a lot of them really wanted younger workers on the floor because they could get away with paying them less, since the younger workers have less experience." When she lost her job again in mid–2008, she decided enough was enough. "I was lucky that I got a decent severance package when the company downsized. Between that money and my husband's income, I had enough of a cushion to think hard about my next step. Did I want to keep getting hired and laid off over and over again until I wasn't hirable anymore, or did I want to find a job that I could keep working at until I retire without all these bumps in the road?" The problem, as she saw it, was that manufacturing had been her career for so long she wasn't sure what else she could do. "I kept seeing plants and factories closing down all over Dallas and Fort Worth and didn't know what kind of options would be left for me. I don't mind telling you I was a little scared about that."

Anna had been out of work for nearly three months when she passed a construction site while driving to a friend's house in the nearby suburbs. "The sign at the site said it was going to be the headquarters of a wind power company," she says. "It had to have been at least the third or fourth wind power company I noticed opening up recently. That got me thinking. The factories were all shutting down or firing workers, but these wind companies just kept popping up everywhere like wildflowers. I'd already seen all those giant wind turbines at the Horse Hollow Wind Energy Center in Nolan on the news, and I thought to myself, 'Well, someone's got to build those darn things, right?' I figured I worked with metal all my life, so why not me?"

She discussed her idea with her husband. "He had no idea what the heck I was talking about," Anna laughs. "He kept calling them windmills!"

world a better, cleaner place for my kids and, hopefully one day, my grandchildren."

Anna's advice for workers looking to transition into the green energy industry is simple. "Just be good at what you do," she says. "That's always been my motto, and I guess it applies to any industry. They hired me even though I had never built a wind turbine in my life, but I'd been in manufacturing for 20 years, so I knew what I was doing and I knew how to do it well. They recognized that and took me on." She also recommends finding out if the state where you live is investing in green energy businesses. "I think most states are now, but if yours isn't, I'd really recommend moving to one that does if you're looking for this kind of job. This is still kind of a new industry, and the states that are helping it develop the way Texas is are the ones that are really going to benefit from all the new jobs and businesses."

CHAPTER 5

GOVERNMENT

When we think of the government, the first thing that usually springs to mind is our elected representatives. It certainly isn't the government as a source of jobs. And yet you might have noticed in the previous chapters just how many of the occupations mentioned are employed by federal, state, and local governments. That's because the government is actually the nation's largest employer, employing about 2.1 percent of the country's entire workforce. In fact, the federal, state, and local government workforce has been growing at an astonishing rate, projected to increase roughly 4.8 percent by 2016, climbing from 10.8 million jobs in 2006 to an estimated 11.3 million.

Even during the recession, government hiring has stayed steady. According to the Department of Labor, the government added 97,000 jobs in 2008 alone, and there's no sign of a slowdown.

Federal Government

The federal government is experiencing growth of all occupations across the board—the only exception being postal service workers, who are expected to see a 2 percent *decrease* in

employment by 2016, due to e-mail, private delivery companies, and greater overall efficiencies in the processing and sorting of mail that will require fewer workers. Still, with a workforce of 1.8 million civilian employees (not including certain agencies whose employment data isn't released to the public for national security reasons, such as the CIA, NSA, Defense Intelligence Agency, and National Geospatial-Intelligence Agency) and, as the nation's most diversified employer, with positions in more than 2,000 separate job categories, federal employment is a great source of job stability. The good news for workers all around the country is that, contrary to popular belief, 9 out of 10 employees of every federal cabinet department and independent agency actually work *outside* the Washington, D.C., metro area. In fact, only 8 percent of federal employees work in D.C., while 39 percent work in the South, 21 percent in the West, 13 percent in the Midwest and 12 percent in the Northeast. Other factors that make government employment so attractive are its often flexible schedule, its stability—the federal government isn't affected by cyclical fluctuations in the economy the way many private sector industries are—and the fact that the jobs tend to have unparalleled benefit packages, including a great retirement and health-care plan, generous paid vacations, assistance with tuition and paying off student loans, and possibly even long-term care insurance. But there are hidden benefits, too, not the least of which is the fact that these days federal government workers are interacting with the private sector more than ever, which means workers are building new skills and connections that can help them return to the private sector in the future, should they want to do so.

According to the U.S. Office of Personnel Management, the current number of civilian jobs in cabinet departments and independent agencies break down to some impressive figures:

- Department of Defense: 688,000 employees
- Department of Veterans Affairs: 246,000 employees
- Department of Homeland Security: 169,000 employees
- Department of Justice: 128,000 employees
- Department of the Treasury: 123,000 employees
- Department of Agriculture: 103,000 employees
- Department of Health and Human Services: 88,000 employees
- Department of the Interior: 73,000 employees
- Social Security Administration: 64,000 employees
- Department of Transportation: 62,000 employees
- Department of Commerce: 60,000 employees
- Department of State: 26,000 employees
- Environmental Protection Agency: 23,000 employees
- Department of Labor: 22,000 employees
- National Aeronautics and Space Administration (NASA): 22,000 employees
- Department of Energy: 20,000 employees
- General Services Administration: 16,000 employees
- Tennessee Valley Authority: 12,000 employees
- Department of Housing and Urban Development: 13,000 employees
- Department of Education: 7,000 employees
- Small Business Administration: 7,000 employees
- Office of Personnel Management: 7,000 employees
- Other, smaller agencies combined: 75,000 employees

Although the federal government employs workers in every major occupational group, the analytical and technical nature of many government duties translates into a much higher proportion of professional, management, business, and financial occupations compared to most private-sector industries, and consequently a much smaller proportion of workers

in occupations the government has less need of, such as sales workers, since the government does very little sales.

The highest percentage of federal government workers, 33.2 percent, are in management, business, and financial occupations. These include the following:

- Compliance officers, who compose 4.6 percent of all workers
- Management analysts, who compose 2.3 percent
- Claims adjusters, examiners, and investigators, who compose 2.2 percent
- Tax examiners, collectors, and revenue agents, who compose 1.8 percent
- General and operations managers, who compose 1.5 percent
- Purchasing agents, who compose 1.5 percent
- Human resources, training and labor relations specialists, who compose 1.2 percent
- Logisticians (who analyze and coordinate the logistical functions of an organization or project), who compose 1.2 percent
- Accountants and auditors, who compose 1.2 percent
- Budget analysts, who compose 0.7 percent
- Financial managers, who compose 0.6 percent

Almost as large is the number of workers in professional and related occupations, who make up 32.8 percent of all federal employees. These include the following:

- Engineers, who compose 4.6 percent of all workers
- Computer specialists, who compose 3.9 percent
- Registered nurses, who compose 2.7 percent
- Health technologists and technicians, who compose 2.1 percent

- Lawyers, who compose 1.6 percent
- Education, training, and library workers, who compose 1.6 percent
- Engineering technicians, who compose 1.5 percent
- Physicians and surgeons, who compose 1.3 percent
- Forest and conservation technicians, who compose 1.3 percent
- Biological scientists, who compose 1.2 percent
- Paralegals and legal assistants, who compose 0.7 percent
- Licensed practical and vocational nurses, who compose 0.7 percent
- Biological technicians, who compose 0.6 percent
- Conservation scientists, who compose 0.4 percent
- Chemists, who compose 0.3 percent
- Environmental scientists and specialists, who compose 0.3 percent
- Occupational health and safety specialists, who compose 0.3 percent

Following the professional occupations, the next largest occupational group in the federal government is office and administrative support, which accounts for 14.3 percent of all employees. These include the following:

- Secretaries and administrative assistants, who compose 1.7 percent of all workers
- Government program eligibility interviewers (who determine whether applicants are eligible to receive assistance from government programs and agency resources like welfare and social security), who compose 1.3 percent
- Bookkeeping, accounting, and auditing clerks, who compose 1.1 percent
- Procurement clerks, who compose 0.7 percent

- Human resource assistants, who compose 0.7 percent
- Word processors and typists, who compose 0.7 percent

Service occupations make up 8 percent of federal employment. These include the following:

- Detectives and criminal investigators, who compose 2 percent of all workers
- Corrections officers and jailers, who compose 0.8 percent
- Police/sheriff's patrol officers, who compose 0.6 percent
- Building cleaning workers, who compose 0.6 percent
- Firefighters, who compose 0.4 percent

(We'll be taking a more in-depth look at roles like police officers and detectives in the next chapter, "Security.")

Installation, maintenance, and repair occupations make up 4.7 percent of employees, with aircraft mechanics and service technicians composing 1 percent, and electrical and electronic equipment mechanics, installers, and repairers composing 0.8 percent. Transportation occupations employ 2.9 percent of federal workers, with air traffic controllers composing 1.1 percent. Lastly, farming, fishing, and forestry occupations make up 0.4 percent of employees, mostly agricultural inspectors, who compose 0.3 percent of all federal workers.

A 2009 report by the nonprofit Partnership for Public Service claims that between then and 2011, the federal government is projected to hire nearly 193,000 new employees to fill mission-critical government jobs in almost every occupational field. The report finds that roughly 80 percent of the new hires for government jobs will be in five professional fields.

- Security, protection, compliance, and enforcement will compose 62,863 new hires, including inspectors,

investigators, police officers, security and prison guards, airport screeners, customs and border patrol officers, immigration agents, and intelligence analysts (we'll be looking at kinds of roles more in the next chapter).

- Medical and public health will compose 35,350 new hires, including doctors, nurses, nursing assistants, pharmacists, medical technicians, occupational therapists, and industrial hygienists, as well as related professionals like health insurance specialists and claims and customer service representatives to implement the Department of Health and Human Services' Medicare Prescription Drug Benefit.

- Accounting, budget, and business will compose 21,248 new hires, including accountants, auditors, budget and financial analysts, and contracting specialists for the Federal Reserve and other financial agencies that enforce regulations, as well as revenue agents and tax examiners needed by the Internal Revenue Service.

- Engineering and sciences will compose 17,477 new hires, including engineers of all disciplines, as well as microbiologists, botanists, physicists, chemists, and veterinarians; the Pentagon alone hired 7,652 engineers in 2009, and the Nuclear Regulatory Commission expects to hire up to 500 professionals in these fields annually for the next several years.

- Program management/analysis and administration will compose 14,305 new hires, including program managers and skilled analysts who monitor program operations, and administrative staff.

Other areas of increasing demand include air traffic controllers (15,004 hired in 2009), foreign service officers (3,500 hired), and patent examiners (1,500 hired).

Driving the federal government hiring rush is the impending retirement of some 550,000 federal workers in the next five years. The U.S. Office of Personnel Management (OPM) estimates that among all full-time permanent employees in the federal government workforce, 58 percent of supervisory and 42 percent of nonsupervisory workers will be eligible to retire by the end of 2010. The resulting windfall of job openings and job growth means that more than just the five professions highlighted in the previous list will be benefiting from government hires. Of course, turnover will affect some agencies and occupations more than others. For example, OPM's projections through 2010 show a disproportionate number of workers will become eligible for retirement at the Department of Housing and Urban Development (48.3 percent), the Federal Aviation Administration (47.1 percent), and the Social Security Administration (40.0 percent). Therefore, it won't come as any surprise that the predominant occupations in these three agencies—air traffic controllers, social insurance administrators, and general business and industry specialists like claims representatives and contracting specialists—are in proportionally high demand through 2010.

The same applies to information technology (IT) workers. According to the federal government's Chief Information Officers Council, the IT community will be hit hard by a retirement wave by 2010. Government agencies are already reporting dramatically increased demand for IT specialists. In 2007, two out of every three agencies listed IT as a mission-critical occupation, and in 2009, the government hired an additional 11,562 IT professionals.

Finance professionals and analysts who lost their Wall Street jobs will find phenomenal opportunities to use their existing skill sets in stable, secure careers in a wide variety of federal government agencies, ranging from the FDIC (Federal Deposit

Insurance Corporation) to the FBI to the SEC (Securities and Exchange Commission). That's certainly good news for the estimated 100,000 workers who are projected to lose their jobs in the financial sector by the second quarter of 2010. The SEC, criticized in the past couple of years for having too many lawyers and not enough analysts as it failed to prevent the recession or unearth Bernard Madoff's Ponzi scheme, is particularly in the market for finance analysts as they seek to increase their efficiency and regain their credibility by bringing in the much more current and useful skill sets offered by ex-Wall Streeters.

Even as the federal government distributes money to create jobs as part of the Recovery Act, it is creating jobs within the government. This is especially true in the areas that the Obama administration has prioritized: energy, environment, health care, and education. But the great majority of these jobs will come with the federal government's infrastructure maintenance initiative targeting airports, highways, bridges, rail lines, power facilities, military facilities, veterans medical centers, and waste and water systems. As the plan comes online, it will generate a massive amount of new construction and engineering jobs available through the government, and so will the $4 billion in Recovery Act funds that the Department of Housing and Urban Development plans to use for improvements to thousands of public housing units nationwide. And, as mentioned in the previous chapter, none of these infrastructure jobs can be outsourced or done off-site. The money spent on these projects will remain within the U.S. economy, boosting it and, in turn, creating more jobs in other hard hit sectors that rely on a strong economy.

Another positive career aspect of so many new government jobs being created by Recovery Act projects all over the country is that it takes manpower to oversee the spending plans and

enforce new rules and regulations, resulting in a rapidly escalating need for managers in human resources and public affairs,
as well as regulators, accountants, and administrators. Experienced workers looking to make a career change into the federal
government will find themselves in good company, too. Nearly
half the people hired by the federal government are experienced
workers over the age of 35.

Education and training requirements for federal jobs are
pretty much the same as those in the private sector, albeit with
some small but important differences. First, obviously, applicants for all but a very small handful of government jobs must
be U.S. citizens. For jobs requiring access to sensitive or classified materials, applicants must undergo a background check,
covering the applicant's criminal, credit, and employment history, as well as other records, in order to obtain security clearance. These checks tend to be performed more rigorously than
background checks in the private sector are. Lastly, civil
service exams are required for specific occupations, including
secretarial and clerical, air traffic control, law enforcement, and
certain entry-level jobs. The great majority of government jobs,
though—approximately 80 percent of them—do not require
the exam.

For those concluding their service in the armed forces during the recession, facing a bleak job market can be a brutal
welcome home. However, the federal government offers
many opportunities for military veterans. In fact, applicants
who are veterans may be able to claim veteran's preference,
which gives them preferred status over other candidates with
equal qualifications, as well as assistance with relocation if
necessary. Additionally, the Veterans' Employment Opportunity Act (VEOA) allows veterans to apply for jobs that
are otherwise only open to federal employees and not the
general public.

State and Local Governments

The federal workforce has been growing at a faster rate than state and local governments' labor pool, but states, cities, and counties are adding a greater number of jobs because they employ more than 8 million workers—four times as many as the federal government—with local governments employing more than twice as many workers as state governments, 69.8 percent compared to 30.2 percent. The advantages of working for state or local government tend to be similar to those of working for the federal government: stability, growth, and the fact that employer-provided benefits are more common for state and local government employees than they are for workers in the private sector.

While the majority of federal jobs were in management, business, and financial occupations, in state and local government it's service occupations that lead the way, making up 31.3 percent of jobs. These include the following:

- Police/sheriff's patrol officers, who compose 7.7 percent of all workers, the highest of all the jobs in state and local government
- Correctional officers and jailers, who compose 5.1 percent
- Firefighters, who compose 3.4 percent
- Building cleaning workers, who compose 1.4 percent
- Nursing, psychiatric, and home health aides, who compose 1.3 percent
- Recreation workers, who compose 1.3 percent
- Landscaping and groundskeeping workers, who compose 1.1 percent
- Supervisors/managers of police and detectives, who compose 1 percent
- Detectives and criminal investigators, who compose 0.8 percent

- Crossing guards, who compose 0.6 percent
- Supervisors/managers of correctional officers, who compose 0.5 percent
- Lifeguards, ski patrol, and other recreational protective service workers, who compose 0.5 percent
- Gaming services workers, who compose 0.4 percent

The next largest segment of local and state government employment is professional and related occupations, which makes up 20.6 percent of jobs. These include the following:

- Social workers, who compose 2.2 percent of all workers
- Computer specialists, who compose 1.8 percent
- Health technologists and technicians, who compose 1.5 percent
- Registered nurses, who compose 1.1 percent
- Lawyers, who compose 1.1 percent
- Probation officers and correctional treatment specialists, who compose 1.1 percent
- Social and human service assistants (who include social work assistants, residential counselors, alcoholism or drug abuse counseling aides, and child abuse workers), who compose 1.1 percent
- Counselors, who compose 0.9 percent
- Library technicians, who compose 0.8 percent
- Civil engineers, who compose 0.7 percent
- Legal support workers, who compose 0.7 percent
- Librarians, who compose 0.6 percent
- Civil engineering technicians, who compose 0.5 percent
- Urban and regional planners, who compose 0.3 percent
- Judges and magistrates, who compose 0.3 percent

Office and administrative support occupations make up 19.6 percent of all jobs in state and local government. These include the following:

- General office clerks, who compose 4 percent of all workers
- Secretaries and administrative assistants, who compose 3.8 percent
- Bookkeeping, accounting, and auditing clerks, who compose 1.3 percent
- Court, municipal, and license clerks, who compose 1.3 percent
- Police, fire, and ambulance dispatchers, who compose 1.1 percent
- Government program eligibility interviewers, who compose 1 percent
- Library assistants, who compose 0.8 percent

Management, business and financial occupations make up 11.7 percent of all jobs. They include the following:

- Accountants and auditors, who compose 1 percent of all workers
- General and operations managers, who compose 0.9 percent
- Human resources, training and labor relations specialists, who compose 0.9 percent
- Legislators, who, it might surprise you to learn, only compose 0.8 percent of all state and local government workers
- Compliance officers, who compose 0.7 percent
- Tax examiners, collectors, and revenue agents, who compose 0.6 percent
- Real estate appraisers and assessors, who compose 0.4 percent

Construction occupations make up 5.6 percent of all jobs. These include the following:

- Highway maintenance workers, who compose 1.7 percent of all workers
- Construction equipment operators, who compose 1 percent

Transportation occupations make up 4.6 percent of all jobs. These include the following:

- Transit and intercity bus drivers, who compose 1.5 percent of all workers
- Garbage and recycling collectors, who compose 0.6 percent

The remaining jobs are installation, maintenance, and repair occupations at 3.8 percent, and production occupations at 1.8 percent, including water and liquid waste treatment plant system operators, who compose 1.1 percent of all workers in state and local government.

Among the fastest growing jobs in state and local government are firefighters, which we'll talk more about in Chapter 9. "Dow Busters," and police, which we'll cover in the next chapter.

Also expected to grow rapidly are blue-collar jobs connected to infrastructure, especially with the Recovery Act's infrastructure maintenance initiative. In that same vein, urban and regional planning will see growth, too, as it remains the linchpin in the nation's quest to lower our carbon footprint. Strengthening mass transit systems, limiting sprawl, encouraging use of bicycles, and deemphasizing cars is only part of the urban and regional planning mission. Equally important is contingency planning, as floods, heat waves, and mounting garbage become increasingly common problems for metropolises. Employment in this branch of local government is projected to grow 15 percent by 2016.

When the largest employer in the country is projected to see job growth across the board like this, with only further expansion expected as Recovery Act money is used on projects and programs that will require new workers, it's worth sitting up and taking notice. Job opportunities in just about every occupation are there for the taking in federal, state, and local governments. As mentioned, their application process may be a little more rigorous than you'll find in the private sector, but it's worth it for a stable, long-lasting career in a field where almost any existing skill set is easily transferred. In the appendix, you'll find a comprehensive list of government career resources, including quite a few industry news and job sites, related scholarships, loans and grants, and some helpful guides to help you better understand how to successfully land a government job.

MAKING THE TRANSITION: GOVERNMENT

Dalila H., 42, of Brooklyn, New York, works for the New York City Department of Transportation, a branch of local government that works to provide the safe, efficient, and environmentally responsible movement of people and goods in New York City, and to maintain and enhance the transportation infrastructure that is so crucial to the economic vitality and quality of life of city residents. Though she's been gainfully employed by the NYCDOT for eight years now, working in government wasn't her original career plan.

"I originally went to school to become a teacher," Dalila explains. "This was in Texas, and the state requires that anyone pursuing an education degree take one year of geography. I loved the subject so much I decided to switch my major, thinking I'd become a geography professor. During a geography class, the field of urban planning was mentioned, and I was so excited to learn that people actually *planned* cities that I decided to pursue that as my career." In her pursuit of a master's degree in urban planning, she received help with her expenses through

her school's financial aid program and through work as a graduate assistant. "I was assistant to the Chair of the Planning Department. I did all manner of things from coordinating meetings, editing a newsletter about planning topics, orienting new students, et cetera. I was pretty much his right arm. It provided a stipend that allowed me to undertake one year of study without having to work any other job, so I was very steeped in the academic experience and campus life." The experience also exposed her firsthand to many aspects of the occupation and to working professionals who would become part of her professional network.

Before entering the field of local government, though, Dalila was employed within the private sector by a New York City-based urban planning firm. "We worked for various municipalities in the tri-state region. My role was supportive of the partners in the firm; I did a lot of their due diligence like filling in land-use maps and interviewing local stakeholders to support rezonings or master plans. Prior to that, I worked for a nonprofit and was focused on economic revitalization for a commercial strip in Brooklyn. I did a lot of capacity building with the local merchants: bringing them together to coordinate street fairs and holiday lighting. I worked with the local chamber of commerce to devise a business attraction product to fill vacant stores. And one-on-ones with individual business to help them market their products and apply for loans to stabilize and/or expand their business."

That revitalized commercial strip was Fifth Avenue in Park Slope, Brooklyn, which has since become one of the most vibrant, successful neighborhoods in the borough. But even major success stories like this one couldn't prevent Dalila from losing her job when the economy went bad. "After the post-September 11, 2001, mini-recession, I was laid off from the private-sector firm and needed a job," she says. Being unemployed led her to comb the help-wanted ads for new employment. "I saw the position with the city and thought that would provide more stability."

Dalila feels her transition from the private sector to the public sector was a smooth one. "Obviously, having a degree in urban planning helped, and I needed a few years of experience under my belt to be an

attractive candidate." Before being hired, she went through a background check, which is standard city practice, but didn't have to take the civil servant exam—at least, not right away. "I was hired in a provisional title with the expectation that I'd take a test for a permanent title. I've since done this and have a permanent civil servant title now."

"I was very lucky to get the job when and how I did," Dalila continues. "As a person who now hires people, I can now see that. Right now, there are fewer positions available." With the current job market so anemic, none of her fellow Department of Transportation workers want to risk moving out of their public-sector jobs, which in turn is creating fewer openings. Because she's seen so many personal friends and acquaintances laid off from their jobs, furloughed, or asked to take pay cuts, she's worried that the same will happen to her but admits, "Because I have a permanent title, I do not feel in danger of losing my job, and even though the city is tightening its budget, I still feel secure."

Secure and, just as importantly, feeling fulfilled in her career. "What is satisfying about this government job is that I am able to see a project through from its inception to implementation. Before, I used to just plan things and hope that government or institutions would implement the ideas. Now I conceive of an idea/policy/physical improvement to address an issue and have the tools available to carry it though to a tangible product or change. This is very gratifying."

For workers looking to achieve stable employment in the public sector, Dalila advises starting with internships. "I did many when I was in grad school, and that really helped me understand what the work would be like and built a network of contacts when I became serious about my job search. Learn to work collaboratively and build coalitions; everything in government is a multi-agency/stakeholder effort. The better one is at working within large groups, the more successful and marketable they'll be in government work. Also, if civil servant titles are required, begin taking the tests even before you have a job in government. Being able to say you already have a title when interviewing may tilt the hiring decision in your favor."

CHAPTER 6

SECURITY

In the last chapter, I mentioned a number of federal, state, and local government jobs, such as police officers, prison guards, airport screeners, border patrol agents, and immigration agents, that are part of the government's security sector and worthy of discussion on their own terms. That's because the job market for professionals in the law enforcement, defense, aerospace, and homeland security fields is wide open, and has been ever since 2001. In fact, as we saw in the last chapter, security, protection, compliance, and enforcement lead the field in new government positions—62,863 over the next two years. As the job opportunities in security continue to grow, there simply aren't enough skilled workers to fill them.

With stepped-up efforts to secure the country from terrorism, drug trafficking, and illegal immigration, the Departments of Defense and Homeland Security alone are expected to offer more than 83,000 new jobs this year. More than 15,000 new customs and border patrol agents and 22,000 Transportation Security Agency (TSA) airport screeners will be hired over the next three years. Also among the biggest security employers are the Nuclear Regulatory Commission, Government Accountability Office, Securities and Exchange Commission, NASA, and the Department of Justice.

It's hard to know exactly how many employees there are in federal security, or what exactly all their roles are, because certain agencies don't release their employment data to the public for national security reasons, such as the CIA, National Security Agency (NSA), Defense Intelligence Agency (DIA), and National Geospatial-Intelligence Agency (NGA). However, we do know the DIA claims more than 16,500 military and civilian employees on their Web site, and we also know the NGA had approximately 9,000 employees way back in 1998. But that's as close as any of us can get to this classified information without pulling a Tom Cruise in *Mission: Impossible.* However, some employment numbers and occupations are available for other security agencies and departments through the Partnership for Public Service. For example:

- The Department of Defense employs approximately 8,000 security administrators, 7,000 intelligence analysts, 400 foreign affairs workers, and 200 international relations workers.
- The Department of Homeland Security employs approximately 60,000 transportation security officers, 12,000 border patrol agents, 2,000 police officers, 1,500 security administrators, 1,300 intelligence analysts, 500 asylum officers, and 200 contact representatives.
- The Department of the Interior employs 4,000 park rangers.
- The Department of Justice employs 20,000 correctional officers, 4,000 intelligence analysts, and 1,000 security administrators.
- The Department of Veterans Affairs employs 3,000 police officers.

Today, more than 80 federal organizations employ law enforcement officers and security agents, including the FBI; the Drug Enforcement Administration (DEA); the U.S. Marshals; the Bureau of Alcohol, Tobacco, Firearms, and Explosives (ATF); and the Bureau of Diplomatic Security. Even the Postal Service, the Bureau of Indian Affairs, the Forest Service, and the National Park Service have their own security and law enforcement branches.

But it's in the Department of Homeland Security (DHS) that we can expect to see the most growth. That's because the DHS is one of the largest federal agencies, encompassing several departments where a variety of occupations are in great demand. Because security threats against the nation are constantly changing, from pandemics to hurricanes to terrorism, the DHS offers a diverse career field that cuts across numerous disciplines, creating job possibilities for people with nearly any level of education and experience (though background checks and security clearances are required, as is being a U.S. citizen). Following are some departments and roles within the DHS:

- Citizenship and Immigration Services: Asylum officers and immigration officers
- Customs and Border Protection: Border patrol agents and import specialists
- Federal Emergency Management Agency (FEMA): Coordinating officers and response, recover, preparedness, and mitigation specialists
- Federal Law Enforcement Training Center: Teachers
- Immigration and Customs Enforcement: Detention and deportation officers, police officers, immigration and enforcement agents, and security specialists

- Information Analysis and Infrastructure Protection Directorate: Security advisors, intelligence operations specialists, IT workers, security specialists, and telecommunications specialists
- Office of the Inspector General: Attorneys and auditors
- Science and Technology Directorate: Biological scientists, chemists, computer scientists, engineers, and physicists
- Secretarial Offices: Human resources specialists, policy analysts
- Transportation and Security Administration: Criminal investigators, intelligence operations specialists, program management analysts, and airport security screeners
- U.S. Coast Guard: Contract specialists and engineers
- U.S. Secret Service: Criminal investigators, especially in the fields of counterfeiting, forgery, and credit card fraud

As you can see, it's not all security agents and law enforcement officers who make up the DHS. Other occupations like engineers, teachers, scientists, and lawyers are in demand as well. However, those applicants coming from a law enforcement or analyst background will definitely have an advantage and transition the easiest.

The security sector of government currently employs just under 900,000 workers, 79 percent of which are employed by local governments, such as your neighborhood police precinct. State agencies employ about 11 percent, including state troopers and highway patrol officers, and various federal agencies employ about 7 percent.

Growth is assured in just about all the roles involved in government-level security and law enforcement, at least as far as we can tell from the data that's available to us. Classified data for other agencies may show even more growth than the following numbers, but even without that data the numbers are pretty promising:

- Detectives and criminal investigators are expected to grow by 17 percent by 2016, adding approximately 18,000 workers.
- Police/sheriff's patrol officers by 11 percent, adding 70,000 workers.
- Supervisors/managers of police and detectives by 9 percent, adding 8,500 workers.
- Transit and railroad police by 6 percent, adding 400 workers.
- Fish and game wardens is the only security occupation expected to see 0 percent growth forecast, keeping steady at its 8,000 workers.

Employment numbers in related occupations will see increased growth as well, such as the federal, state, and local governments' correctional fields:

- Correctional officers and jailers are expected to grow by 17 percent by 2016, adding approximately 75,000 workers.
- Supervisors/managers of correctional officers by 13 percent, adding 5,000 workers.
- Probation officers and correctional treatment specialists by 11 percent, adding 10,000 workers.
- Bailiffs by 11 percent, adding 2,100 workers.

There are plenty of job opportunities in the armed forces as well, and you don't even have to enlist. Right now the defense sector is looking for employees with the right kind of technical ability and who are eligible for security clearance. For example, just about any defense contractor, military base, or related government agency has a demand for systems engineers, the professionals who design radar and satellite systems, flight control for aircrafts, guidance systems for missiles, and command and control technology. Software developers are also

heavily in demand as more personnel are required to write the programs that guide aircraft and missile systems. Scientists are getting hired, too, with the Navy recently announcing it's looking to bring on about 1,000 new civilian scientist employees—in engineering, physics, chemistry, just about anything related to the sciences—for weapons research and development, and is even willing to train them for the skills they need. Even better, growth in defense manufacturing is leading to an increased need for workers with a wide range of skills, from machinists to clerical workers.

Defense hiring continues to be so strong that students who graduate with degrees in engineering, science, and IT are fielding multiple job offers—even in this job climate. The Missile Defense Agency and companies that frequently get defense and intelligence contracts like Lockheed Martin and Northrop Grumman are experiencing such a mounting need for more skilled professionals that they're actively recruiting employees right off of university campuses.

But the IT crowd isn't just getting hired by defense agencies to create guidance systems. IT workers are seeing opportunities all over the government security sector. A July 2009 report by the Partnership for Public Service in conjunction with consulting company Booz Allen Hamilton found after studying 18 federal agencies that the nation's security could be in jeopardy because not enough workers have been hired who are sufficiently trained to protect computer systems from hackers, criminals, terrorists, and foreign governments. The federal government, the report concludes, is at serious risk of being unable to fight off attacks on the nation's computer networks unless it strengthens its cybersecurity workforce.

President Obama had already labeled the cyber threat one of the most serious economic and national security challenges facing the nation by the time the report came out. In May 2009,

he announced his intention to create the post of cybersecurity coordinator to oversee a new, comprehensive approach to securing the nation's digital infrastructure, including the hiring of more cybersecurity experts for the federal workforce through a new strategy of recruiting, training, and retaining cybersecurity workers. In an effort similar to what previous administrations did during the space race, one part of the proposed strategy will involve reaching out to universities and the private sector to encourage workers to develop technological skills, including college scholarships in the cybersecurity field. Another part of the proposed strategy will be training existing federal workers in state-of-the-art technologies, but even then there won't be enough employees to satisfy the report's warnings. Those workers who get a leg up on cybersecurity now will have a definite advantage of becoming part of the industry's government growth. The report also recommends that the Office of Personnel and Management adjust the often labyrinthine federal hiring process, create a cybersecurity career path, and expedite security clearances, all of which will mean easier and quicker employment for workers in order to address the inadequate supply of potential new IT experts.

Computer specialists in the security sector, especially those with network administration, systems analysis, and programming skills, will be required to analyze data, create, and operate translation software, and break codes. In the law enforcement sector, they will continue to be in high demand, not just because of the proliferation of computer evidence in most modern crimes but also to prevent and combat growing online organized crime. With the security intelligence firm iDefense's 2009 Cyber Threats and Trends report forecasting an increase in malware virus distribution, targeted "phishing" incidents against commercial accounts, the use of fast-flux hosting technology designed to prevent the detection of

malicious sites, online fraud, and risk to banking systems from hackers, law enforcement employees with IT skills on both the local and federal level will be in greater demand than ever before. Similarly, more and more law enforcement agencies are partnering up with IT companies, moving toward the use of online communication to disseminate crime information more quickly and efficiently. Information sharing networks specifically for security and law enforcement are already coming online, offering information-sharing capabilities in real time via mobile software directly to the agent or officer at the point of incident. The more investigative work becomes reliant on advanced software technology, the more IT professionals should find robust employment opportunities.

One of the most interesting transfers of skills I've seen in my career is happening in the security field right now: namely, laid-off financial workers joining the CIA. Much like the civilian federal government is doing, the CIA has decided to capitalize on the financial crisis by launching a recruiting campaign targeting ex-Wall Streeters, running radio and print ads in New York and the financial media. Since a job with the CIA is considerably more stable than a hedge fund these days, the campaign is paying off. The agency estimates it received a total of 180,000 applications in 2009. Filling economic analyst posts with employees who have economic or financial backgrounds is a no-brainer, but the CIA's expansive national security portfolio also includes other topics that applicants with these backgrounds are well suited for, such as counterterrorism, counternarcotics, and counterproliferation—all areas where money has to be tracked and transactions analyzed.

In addition, the CIA is now producing a daily Economic Intelligence Brief for the President, chronicling economic, political, and leadership developments that could impact the world economy in order to make sure that the country isn't taken by

surprise by the implications of the worldwide economic crisis. This too will require strong recruitment of economic analysts. While working for the CIA is bound to be a very different use of financial industry workers' skill sets than they used on Wall Street, the main attraction here is how easily their existing skills translate over to a stable, growing employment field, not to mention one that happens to be serving their country instead of just the bottom line.

On a local level, there is always a demand for more police officers. A more security-conscious society and concern about drug-related crimes, especially during economic downturns, is fueling an increasing demand for police services. Because law enforcement officers can retire with a pension after 25 or 30 years of service, allowing them to pursue a second career while still in their 40s or 50s, layoffs in law enforcement are rare and most staffing cuts are handled through attrition. What's more, the few trained law enforcement officers who do lose their jobs because of budget cuts usually have no difficulty finding jobs with other agencies or even private security firms. The need to replace workers who retire, transfer to other occupations, or stop working for other reasons will be the source of many job openings. (Applicants who have served in the military may be eligible for additional benefits, like counting their years in the service toward their years with the department for retirement and pension purposes.)

The news gets even better for law enforcement applicants; the federal government, as part of the Recovery Act, plans to give $1 billion in grants to law enforcement agencies throughout the country to help pay for the hiring and rehiring of officers by state, local, and tribal governments. The Department of Justice received more than 7,200 applications for more than 39,000 officer positions this year, representing a total of $8.3 billion in requested funding, an amount that truly reflects the tremendous

demand for new officers. These grants would be distributed on top of the $4 billion in Department of Justice grant funding already distributed as part of the Recovery Act to local law enforcement, some of which has already been disbursed to states to help crime victims, including women who are targets of violence, to fight Internet crimes against children, and to meet other law enforcement needs.

The current round of grants, to be administered by the Department of Justice's Office of Community Oriented Policing Services (COPS), will be awarded to 1,046 law enforcement agencies in all 50 states, and will provide 100 percent of the approved salary and benefits for 4,699 officers for three years, with police departments that receive the money agreeing to retain the grant-funded positions for an additional year after that.

Funding decisions were based on crime reports for the previous calendar year; community policing activities; budget changes; and poverty, unemployment, and foreclosure rates in the area, so that the new officers can go to the places where they're needed the most. For example, Pennsylvania, one of the hardest hit states in terms of economic decline, plans to create or save 93 law enforcement positions statewide by awarding more than $20 million to 19 law enforcement agencies. Philadelphia alone, where more than 19 percent of families live below the poverty line and where the unemployment rate rose from 6.4 percent in 2008 to 8.8 percent in 2009, will be able to create or preserve 50 additional law enforcement jobs.

Between the retiring workforce and the government funding grants, there has never been a better time to enter the law enforcement field than right now. It may not be the right job for everyone—being a police officer or detective can be dangerous and stressful work—but there are certain appealing benefits that make it an attractive option, such as job stability,

the opportunity for upward mobility through the ranks, and a robust pension plan for retirement.

Private-Sector Opportunities

Security also happens to be one biggest areas of private-sector employment as well. Many establishments throughout the country are now being made more secure, and as a result, new opportunities for security workers have popped up everywhere from seaports to shopping centers. Hotels, health-care facilities, and almost any business of substantial size employ security personnel. So do educational institutions, who require college campus security, as well as rail transportation, private investigation firms, private security companies, and casinos, where security workers are known as gaming surveillance officers.

Security guards and gaming surveillance officers currently hold over 1 million jobs in the United States. More than half of all jobs for security guards were in investigation and security services, including guard and armored car services, that provide security on a contract basis to buildings and other sites as needed. Most other security guards are employed directly by educational institutions, hospitals, hotels, department stores, manufacturing firms, and residential and non-residential buildings. Employment of security guards is expected to grow by 17 percent by 2016, adding a projected 175,000 employees to the field as the need for security continues to increase due to concerns about crime, vandalism, and terrorism. Demand for security guards will see further growth as private security firms are increasingly relied on to provide security at public events and in some residential neighborhoods.

Gaming surveillance officers, on the other hand, work primarily in casinos and casino hotels, though some also work directly with local governments in states and on Indian reservations where gambling is legal. Employment of gaming surveillance officers is expected to grow by an amazing 34 percent by 2016, adding an additional 2,900 workers. This growth is being spurred by casinos hiring more surveillance officers as more states legalize gambling and as the number of casinos in states where gambling is already legal grows.

As our nation's security needs increase in both the public and private sectors, the field remains a steady source of job growth for workers with a wide variety of skills and, in some cases, the ability to pass a rigorous background check for security clearance. Ever since the terrorist attacks of 2001, the security job market has been growing rapidly, leading the way in new government hires and offering many opportunities for career longevity. In the appendix, you'll find a comprehensive list of security career resources, including certification courses; industry information and job sites; information on how to apply for related grants, scholarships, and loans; and where to download an informative guide from American Society for Industrial Security (ASIS) International called "Career Opportunities in Security."

MAKING THE TRANSITION: SECURITY

When Neil E., 48, of Springfield, Virginia, lost his job as a program manager at an online media firm in Des Moines, Iowa, the last place he expected to find a new job was with the Customs and Border Protection (CPB) agency of the U.S. Department of Homeland Security. "The company I worked for in Des Moines was acquired by a much larger firm that already had their own program managers that they wanted to keep on, even though I actually had more experience

than most of them, so they let me go as redundant," he says. "After I was laid off, I was at a loss. I knew I had extremely marketable skills and businesses should have been beating down my door to hire me, but I kept bumping up against hiring freezes and a glutted job market filled with people who were willing to take a position for a lot less pay than I was."

Neil's path to a job in the security sector came about more by accident than design. "I met a friend for breakfast one day, and he showed me a story in the newspaper about how the Department of Homeland Security was looking to hire tons of people in all kinds of positions. He thought I should check it out, but I was skeptical at first. I figured those jobs were for tough guys who hunt down terrorists or inspect cargo for bombs, not people like me who develop and track business performance metrics, or train project teams to use specialized software."

Still, facing a dry job market with few prospects, he decided to look into it by doing some research online, including visiting government career job boards. It was on the USAJOBS site that he discovered that Customs and Border Protection had an opening for a program manager. Neil decided it couldn't hurt to apply. "I've always been self-motivated, so I took a 'let's see what happens' approach and followed through," he says. "I learned very quickly that applying for a government job is quite different from applying for a job in the private sector. It's more complicated, for one thing. The job titles are standardized, so you kind of have to be flexible about titles and search a little deeper. I found a lot of jobs with different responsibilities all listed under the same title. But what was helpful was that the job qualifications were much more specific in the government listings than I was used to seeing in private-sector ads. I had to make my résumé much more detailed than before, too. They wanted me to be very specific about my experience, who I worked with, who I reported to, and how my work was used. It was like answering all the usual job interview questions right up front. They also use a system I had never seen before where they classify positions

numerically according to what sort of duties are involved." This is the General Schedule (GS) system, a classification structure that almost had Neil throwing up his hands in frustration before he dug a little deeper. "It was actually easier to figure out than I originally thought," he admits. "The job I applied for was listed as a GS–13, and it turned out that the amount of experience and education I already had qualified me for a position of that level."

After filling out an occupational questionnaire, taking part in several rigorous interviews, and undergoing a background security check that Neil describes as "thorough and lengthy, but not too painful," Customs and Border Protection offered Neil the program manager job, but there was still one hurdle left to jump. He lived in Des Moines, and the job was located in Springfield, Virginia. "I knew the job was in Virginia from the start," he explains, "but since I was originally just applying for the job to see what would happen and part of me never thought I'd get it, I suddenly found myself with a big decision on my hands. Namely, should I stay in Iowa and keep looking for work there or move to Virginia?" A number of factors helped push him toward making the move. "I'm not married and don't have the needs of a family to consider, so my roots in Des Moines weren't planted as deep as they might be for other people faced with a similar decision. The absolute dearth of job opportunities wasn't doing much to keep me there either." But it was the Customs and Border Protection agency itself that finally convinced him to relocate by making a generous offer. "I was relieved and more than a little flattered when they said they would pay for my relocation expenses. That was the icing on the cake."

Neil says he is more than satisfied with the job after being able to translate his skills into a new field. "I'm very happy I accepted the job with the CBP. I've always enjoyed problem solving, team building, and developing and managing resources, and I still get to do that, just for a different organization with a different mission. I've always loved a good challenge too, and there's no shortage of those here. I think the most

challenging and often the most rewarding part of my job is when I get to identify and resolve issues where there's no existing policy yet, which allows me to be innovative and take the initiative. It's especially satisfying when my implementations are taken under consideration by the top-level managers as possible new agencywide policies. My job also gives me the opportunity to interact on a regular basis with high-ranking officials in other federal agencies. It really feels like I'm making a difference." Furthermore, Neil hasn't felt like his job was in danger during the recession. "Absolutely not. In fact, I'm seeing just as many people being hired by Homeland Security now as there was when the recession first started. Another good thing I can say about working for the federal government is that my job isn't in any danger from corporate acquisition anymore. No one's going to buy the Department of Homeland Security and lay me off as redundant."

While Neil recommends a job in the security sector for anyone looking for a new, stable career, he admits that competition can be fierce for some positions. "In the federal government, most job openings are made available to the public, but they tend to do a lot of merit promoting from within to fill the higher positions with existing federal employees. Veterans are given preference for a lot of jobs as well. I consider myself very lucky to have gotten such a high-level job as an outsider and as someone who never served in the armed forces. Also, you really have to know how to work well with others and not get too frustrated by stressful situations; otherwise, you'll burn out quickly. The bureaucracy in government can be unbelievable, and Customs and Border Protection is no exception. Sometimes you really have to push for what you need, even if it's something as important as recommendations for program improvements, because things tend to move at a glacial speed and you'll often find a stubborn resistance to changes to the status quo. I suppose that's not so different from working for any organization in the private sector, really, but if you can handle bureaucracy and aren't afraid to keep pushing for what you want, you'll do fine."

CHAPTER 7

INFORMATION TECHNOLOGY

By now you might have noticed there is one occupational field that has appeared in each and every growth industry mentioned in this book: information technology, namely, anything having to do with computers, software, and the Internet. We saw it in health care, where President Obama's push to get health-care records digitized is generating an increased demand that could create 50,000 new tech jobs. We saw it in biotechnology, where computer specialists composed 3.2 percent of the industry as a whole. We saw it in education as one of the occupations educational institutions is continuing to hire to prepare students for the needs of the twenty-first-century job market. We saw it in energy, where computer specialists composed 1.3 percent of the traditional oil and coal extraction industry, one of the few roles expected to show any job growth by 2016, and found software developers in particularly high demand for the green energy industry to design and maintain the system that underpins wind farms, smart energy grids, and other green energy systems. We saw it in government, where computer specialists composed 3.9 percent of the total federal workforce, with an additional 11,562 IT professionals set to be hired in 2009, and 1.8 percent of the total state and local workforce. We saw it in

security, where computer specialists were a main component of the Department of Homeland Security's Information Analysis and Infrastructure Protection Directorate and the Science and Technology Directorate, and in defense, where software developers are in high demand to write the programs that guide aircraft and missile systems, and in law enforcement, where their help in battling cybercrimes and recovering computer evidence is invaluable.

Areas that employers deem critical to their survival rarely get cut, even in a recession, and these days there are fewer critical areas than IT. IT workers tend to be shielded from layoffs because a weak economy puts them in special demand. Companies generally have to keep spending on technology to stay competitive, and they want to get the most return on their investment that they can. While it's true that some IT positions have moved overseas in recent years, critical jobs that involve configuring hardware and software remain difficult to outsource because those workers need to be readily available with instant access to critical data.

As a nation, we are relying more heavily on high-tech advances than ever before, with computer technology reaching into every corner of almost every industry, from our cell phones to our kitchen appliances, even our cars. In the business world, retailers, banks, corporations, schools, hospitals— basically any enterprise with records to keep—all need computing power. As a result, IT positions are a plentiful and expanding job market, projected to grow as a whole by more than 24 percent by 2016.

The only problem is that there isn't enough fresh talent coming in to fill the demand, especially as the baby boomers retire from the industry. Across all levels of business, government, and not-for-profit organizations, chief information officers and human resource managers are battling an IT talent shortage. Part

of this is because, as the Government Accountability Office (GAO) found in a study conducted between 1994 and 2004, the proportion of postsecondary students obtaining degrees in science, technology, engineering, and mathematics fields has fallen, primarily because of fears of another dot-com collapse like we had in 2001 and worries about outsourcing, but also because, as a Computer Science Teachers Association survey discovered, there has been a 5 percent decline in high schools that offer introductory computer science courses, and an 8 percent drop in high schools that offer advanced courses in computer science.

Public, private, and governmental organizations, and others in the business and academic communities are collectively trying to increase the visibility of the IT talent demand and rally investments in the future IT workforce, with the particular goal of extinguishing the misperception that the only future for IT is through offshore or outsourced talent. Still, the current lack of competition is great news that workers looking to make the switch from another career into the IT industry can capitalize on.

Another reason for the discrepancy between worker supply and demand is that IT, for whatever reason, has long been thought of as an all-boys club. As a result of this misperception, the IT industry is currently looking to increase its gender diversity. In 1983, women made up approximately 43 percent of the IT workforce, but by 2008, while total IT employment more than doubled, the percentage of female workers had dropped to 26 percent. To help put this in perspective, consider that women represent approximately 46 percent of administrative, science, and technical workers, and approximately 42 percent of all other occupations. Because of the industry's current workforce needs, a number of pilot efforts have been taken in the last few years to lure female, as well as minority, workers into IT, which they

expect will not only help expand their employment numbers to meet their current demand but will also bring a broader range of experience and interests that could stimulate the important creativity that drives the industry to research and develop new technologies and applications.

There is no universal definition of the IT workforce because the industry is actually made up of a number of different, semi-independent fields, all of which are expected to show impressive growth by 2016. These include the following:

- Network systems and data communication analysts, whose employment numbers are expected to grow by a staggering 53 percent, adding approximately 140,000 new jobs to the field
- Computer applications software engineers, who are expected to grow by 45 percent, adding 226,000 new jobs
- Database administrators, who are expected to grow by 29 percent, adding 34,000 new jobs
- Computer systems analysts, who are expected to grow by 29 percent, adding 146,000 new jobs
- Computer systems software engineers, who are expected to grow by 28 percent, adding 99,000 new jobs
- Network and computer systems administrators, who are expected to grow by 27 percent, adding 83,000 jobs
- Computer scientists, who are expected to grow by 22 percent, adding 5,400 new jobs
- Computer and information systems managers, who are expected to grow by 16 percent, adding 43,000 new jobs
- General computer specialists, who are expected to grow by 15 percent, adding 21,000 new jobs
- Computer support specialists (tech support), who are expected to grow by 13 percent, adding 71,000 new jobs
- Computer hardware engineers, who are expected to grow by 5 percent, adding 3,600 new jobs

Look at those numbers again. That's 872,000 new jobs created in the next six years, all in IT.

The Bureau of Labor Statistics is forecasting a 4 percent *decrease* in computer programming employment due to outsourcing and easy to use consumer-end programming software, but don't let that number fool you. Every computer, from the biggest, most complex storage system to the simplest plug-and-play laptop, needs to be programmed, and job opportunities for computer programmers actually remain strong within the computer system design industry.

Employment in computer system designs is projected to grow by an impressive 38.3 percent and has room for a wide variety of workers, not just the computer savvy. Though, as you might expect, the leading occupations in computer system designs, 61.5 percent of all employees, are in professional and related fields. These include the following:

- Computer applications software engineers, who compose 12.4 percent of all workers
- Computer programmers, who compose 10.4 percent
- Computer systems analysts, who compose 7.8 percent
- Computer systems software engineers, who compose 7.3 percent
- Computer support specialists, who compose 6.7 percent
- Network and computer systems administrators, who compose 3.6 percent
- Network systems and data communications analysts, who compose 2.7 percent
- Database administrators, who compose 1.3 percent
- Computer hardware engineers, who compose 1.2 percent
- Market research analysts, who compose 0.7 percent
- Electrical and electronics engineers, who compose 0.6 percent
- Engineering technicians, who compose 0.6 percent

- Graphic designers, who compose 0.6 percent
- Technical writers, who compose 0.6 percent
- Computer scientists, who compose 0.5 percent

Management, business and financial occupations make up 16.7 percent of employment. These include the following:

- Computer and information systems managers, who compose 3.1 percent of all workers
- General and operations managers, who compose 2.4 percent
- Management analysts, who compose 2.2 percent
- Human resources, training and labor relations specialists, who compose 1.4 percent
- Marketing and sales managers, who compose 1.2 percent
- Accountants and auditors, who compose 1.2 percent
- Financial managers, who compose 0.6 percent
- Engineering managers, who compose 0.5 percent

Office and administrative support occupations make up 13 percent of employment. These include the following:

- Customer service representatives, who compose 2.6 percent of all workers
- Secretaries and administrative assistants, who compose 2.5 percent
- Office clerks, who compose 2.2 percent
- Bookkeeping, accounting, and auditing clerks, who compose 1.2 percent

Sales and related occupations make up 6.3 percent of employment. These include the following:

- Sales representatives for services, who compose 2.2 percent of all workers

- Sales representatives for products, who compose 1.9 percent
- Sales engineers, who compose 0.7 percent

Installation, maintenance, and repair occupations make up the remaining 1.5 percent of employment, including computer repairers, who compose 0.7 percent of all workers.

The computer systems design industry grew dramatically throughout the 1990s, when employment more than doubled. Despite the current recession, it still remains among the 10 industries in the nation with the largest job growth, with more than 489,000 new jobs expected to be created by 2016. An increasing reliance on IT combined with the falling prices of computers and related hardware will only continue to spur demand for computer system design. Individuals, businesses, and organizations continue to turn to computer system design firms to maximize their return on investments in equipment and to satisfy their growing computing needs like an increasing reliance on the Internet, faster and more efficient internal and external communication, and the implementation of new technologies and applications.

A number of factors are propelling the IT industry forward. The demand for networking and the need to integrate new hardware, software, and communications technologies is driving demand for widespread IT consulting and integration. A need for more customized applications and for support and services to assist users is driving demand for computer applications software engineers and computer support specialists. The proliferation of mobile technologies and devices like Wi-Fi, BlackBerries, and iPhones have also increased demand for a wide variety of new products and services coming out of the IT field. As businesses and individuals become more dependent on mobile technology, we should see an increased need for "mobility consultants" and service firms that can

design and integrate computer systems so they will be compatible with mobile technologies.

Businesses have started to take note of social media as well. With more and more people reading and partaking in social media venues like blogs, Twitter, MySpace, Facebook, and LinkedIn, social media is becoming a major player in how people communicate and interact, so it's only natural that employers have begun looking for workers with social media expertise, often requiring it of candidates for online marketing jobs. Social media offers businesses the ability to get the word out instantly to a target audience about new products and services, and just as importantly, it offers lightning-fast feedback. While this revolutionary level of online interaction between businesses and consumers doesn't always necessarily lead to groundbreaking success for their products (*Snakes on a Plane*, anyone?), businesses know that instant feedback from a target market can save them a lot of money, negating the old-fashioned practice of releasing a product or service first and then finding out if anyone is interested.

Many businesses know they need to get into social media, but once they're there, they have no idea how to leverage their online existence. As a result, employers have begun hiring people with social networking skills to come on board and take over. The roles for those with social media skills are plentiful and even extend beyond online marketing to occupations like human resources and customer service. For example, the top jobs for workers with social media expertise, according to CareerBuilder.com, include the following:

- *Recruiters.* Job seekers have been scouring social media for job tips for years, but only now have recruiters started to join them. Through social networks, employers have been able to find candidates faster, screen them better, and

reach out to individuals they wouldn't necessarily notice otherwise, such as out-of-towners and telecommuters. Eventually, this online interaction between recruiters and job seekers might even replace the formal interview and screening process.

- *Strategists.* Many employers are looking for social media strategists who can find the best way for their businesses to interact within various social sites and online communities. For instance, forward-thinking companies have been blogging for years, but the rest of the business world is only just now catching up with how important instant communication with consumers can be for the bottom line. The strategist is the social networking face of the company, creating and maintaining an effective social media strategy by interacting with users, growing brand awareness, creating buzz, increasing traffic, and providing valuable information to the marketplace.

- *Enterprise architects.* Never heard of them? That's because this is a relatively new occupation, and one that's increasingly in demand as more and more businesses explore their online potential. Enterprise architects work to link the mission, strategies, and processes of a business to its IT strategy, and then document this by using multiple architectural models that show how their current and future needs will be met in an efficient, sustainable, agile, and adaptable manner. Their goal is to deliver an architecture that supports the most efficient and secure IT environment that meets a company's business needs, especially for those that are looking to revamp their content management strategy and internal networks. This is perhaps the most exciting job in social media today, requiring candidates to have broad experience in networks, multiple platforms, development, and security,

and it could well be the most important role in a company in the next five years.

- *User operations analysts.* Any company with an online presence knows that making sure users have a pleasant and productive experience that will bring them back time and again is one of the most vital parts of the business. Therefore, user experiences need to be monitored to make sure consumers are happy and willing to return. This requires someone, or a team of someones, to be in charge of those experiences. No matter if the company is blogging, has a Web site, or pages on Facebook, MySpace, Twitter, and LinkedIn, user operations analysts are a new breed of the customer service representative, interacting with users, answering queries, investigating problems, and keeping track of user habits.

- *Directors of social media.* Similar to the social media strategists, companies need someone to organize company blogging, viral marketing, podcasting, and all the other social networking options they can take advantage of. A director of social media would have to have a background in building teams, and really understand the promise and the purpose of social media. Directors should be aware of new technologies and be linked in to blogs; have RSS (Really Simple Syndication) feeds; have Facebook, MySpace, and Twitter accounts; and even understand the value of sites like YouTube that are ostensibly only for entertainment purposes but can actually help get the word out about new products and services.

When it comes to employment opportunities in the IT sector, it's all about how up-to-date you are, perhaps more so than in any other profession. Workers who ensure they're current on the newest and best technologies will see the most new job

opportunities and stand a better chance of advancement within the organization, and higher compensation, once they're hired. A report by Robert Half Technology, a leading job placement provider of IT professionals, recently highlighted a number of skills that it predicts will be in particular demand in the years ahead. These include the following:

- *Microsoft .NET development.* As companies increase their investments in application and Web initiatives, workers skilled in developing for the Microsoft .NET framework are in big demand. In fact, some candidates with these skills can command a 10 percent premium over their counterparts without these skills. Expertise in .NET is valued in such positions as Web developer or designer and software developer or engineer.
- *SQL Server development.* The growth of applications and Web development is also fueling the need for SQL Server development skills. Firms need professionals who can write code, including stored procedures, database scripts, and triggers. While some positions focus purely on SQL Server development, often these skills are applied to other roles, such as database administrator, applications architect, and applications developer.
- *Windows administration.* Windows administration knowledge is the technical skill set most in demand in IT departments. It is highly valued in positions such as system administrator, desktop support analyst, and help desk manager. People who can install, configure, and manage ongoing maintenance of Windows servers are typically offered 10 percent more compensation than candidates without the expertise.
- *Network administration.* Network administration skills, particularly experience with Cisco networks, are currently

highly sought after. Network engineer, systems administrator, and telecommunications manager are the types of roles that often require the ability to maintain and troubleshoot Cisco routers, hubs, and switches. Workers with Cisco network administration skills earn an average of 12 percent more than professionals who don't have that training.

- *Database management.* As more businesses recognize the value of keeping their data well organized and secure, they need individuals with the necessary skills to achieve that goal, such as business intelligence analysts, data architects, and database managers—the people who can handle everything from implementation and upgrades to data analysis. Oracle database and Microsoft SQL Server expertise remain in notable demand, with workers commanding salaries at least 10 percent more than candidates without such knowledge.

- *Wireless network management.* As wireless devices, such as tablet PCs, portable e-mail, and smart phones, become more prevalent in the workplace, we're seeing a corresponding increase in the need for professionals with wireless network management abilities. A poll of CIOs shows 52 percent cited these skills as the most sought-after in their IT departments, especially since employees such as messaging administrators and network engineers are helping businesses keep their staff, customers, and clients connected. Wireless network management skills are also critical to ensuring that products are compatible with a business's network and security infrastructure.

The previous chapter covered cybersecurity. Given the growing number of malware and computer viruses out there, the United States is more conscious than ever of the vulnerability

of technology and the Internet. The need for security means an ever-increasing number of IT professionals are finding work with firms that specialize in cyberspace security services, especially custom programmers and designers who can develop antivirus software, programs, and procedures. In fact, a recent study conducted by analyst company IDC found security to be one of the fastest growing areas of IT employment. In 2005, the number of IT security professionals worldwide grew by 9 percent to 1.4 million, almost twice as fast as the rate of growth in other IT professions, and in 2009 that number swelled to 1.9 million, with employers devoting more than 40 percent of their IT security budgets to personnel, including salaries and training.

And yet providers of IT security services are struggling to find suitably qualified candidates. Consequently, though certified specialists will always be first choice for any employer, an increasing number of businesses and organizations are offering their own training programs, a move that is generating even more opportunities for workers looking to move into an information security career. Still, given the fast-changing nature of the threats, and of the role, maintaining accreditation is a continuous process. More than 60 percent of those interviewed by IDC planned to add a further IT security certificate to their portfolios within the next 12 months in order to remain competitive.

CIO.com, a foremost provider of insight and analysis on IT trends for CIOs and other IT leaders, reports that IT security manager is one of the hottest jobs in the industry right now. These are the workers who create and implement corporate IT security practices and ensure their colleagues follow those procedures, consisting of everything from securing Wi-Fi networks and handling off-site storage of backup tapes to establishing policies for lost laptops containing valuable data, and much more.

In July 2009, a financial services company employee named Sergey Aleynikov was arrested by FBI agents for allegedly hacking into his company's computer platform that processes rapid developments in the markets and uses top secret mathematical formulas to allow the firm to make highly profitable automated trades. Recently publicized incidents of system hacks like this one, as well as stolen computers and missing optical disc drives (i.e., CD and DVD burners), all containing confidential records, have driven home an increasing need for businesses to hire workers dedicated to keeping sensitive and important data private. Because the vast amount of information corporate IT systems hold requires protection, security has become a top priority. The security divisions of large technology companies like Microsoft and IBM, as well as security companies like McAfee and Symantec, are all in need of fresh IT security managers to replace the ones who get headhunted away. Federal intelligence agencies are also proving fertile job opportunities for this high-demand role. Overall, IT security managers are projected to see a robust 27 percent growth in employment by 2016.

Independent IT security consultants are also thriving, even in the recession—or maybe because of it. The businesses that manage to do well in tough economic times are often the ones that are flexible and creative, and self-employed consultants have much more freedom in that respect. Provided, of course, that consultants have the reputation, track record, and contacts to find clients, which makes IT security consulting an attractive option for those IT security workers who have been caught up in the layoffs when businesses and organizations downsize, outsource, or close their doors for good. CIOs often look for external help when the services they require lie outside the expertise of in-house staff, or when they need the objective

perspective of someone not embroiled in internal corporate politics. In recessions, they also tend to look for a level of service that they won't get from any of the big information security providers, namely, lower cost, a more personal approach, and more flexibility. For these reasons, a broad base of skills is vital when you are taking the consulting route.

A consultant's qualifications are important, but they are not necessarily the only deciding factors for companies looking to work with them. Just as important is the consultant's approach. Employers want consultants who can listen to their needs and come up with quick, practical solutions. In other words, it's not just how much a consultant knows that sets him or her apart; it's the application of that knowledge. Because consultants must also develop the practical skills needed to run their own businesses, as well as identifying the best advisors in areas such as accounting, taxation, and legal issues, it's not for everyone, but for those who have the self-discipline, motivation, and determination to take on the unpredictable world of freelance, it can be a very successful career shift, especially with so many businesses and organizations focusing on IT security but also looking to save money by turning to consultants. Some consultants even find permanent positions with the companies that hired them for individual projects.

In 2008 the public sector acted as a major area of opportunity for IT security consultants, a trend that is set to continue for the foreseeable future as federal, state, and local governments continue to focus on cybersecurity, and those consultants with a strong track record in this area are now finding themselves tied into longer and more lucrative projects. In the private sector, continued consolidation in the financial services industry is expected to result in an increased demand for consultants with network security and architect skills to assist with

post-merger systems-integration projects. With businesses looking to achieve better security on tighter budgets, they can no longer ignore the growing risk of insider fraud and outside attacks on their systems as economic times get harder. Risk management is more important than ever when companies don't have the financial cushion to bounce back as quickly as they used to, which should make the market strong for those consultants with skills in vulnerability assessment and forensic evaluation.

Compliance also remains an area of nondiscretionary spending for many businesses, creating a lively market for consultants in a variety of information security management systems. Furthermore, as more U.S. companies begin to recognize problems with outsourcing that are likely to affect data security, IT security consultants are poised to pick up the slack as more businesses and organizations bring their security needs back onshore.

IT as a whole has proven itself to be such a vital industry that the Obama administration's Recovery Act has also provided record investments in new technologies. Among them is a recently announced series of grants totaling more than $7.8 million to address IT's growing workforce needs, in an effort to create career pathways into the industry. Among their objectives are exposing more students to the new global workplace and teaching more about IT in today's business culture; retaining present IT workers through new training programs as technology advances; and, in order to reflect the fact that 90 percent of IT workers perform jobs outside the computer industry, offering both IT training and complementary training in business sectors like health care, manufacturing, and financial services. This is on top of more than 200 preexisting federal education programs spending approximately $2.8 billion to promote education and career programs in science,

technology, engineering, and mathematics that are fundamental to the industry.

Related Growth Industries

Just about any industry fueled by computers or the Internet is currently riding the high-tech wave to substantial growth. For example, Internet publishing and broadcasting is estimated to grow by 44.1 percent, wireless communications carriers by 40.9 percent, and software publishing by 32 percent—all of which means more job growth for IT workers. Furthermore, as new technologies continue to come to market, more and more customer service representatives will be needed, spurring a 25 percent employment growth—or about 545,000 new jobs—for that industry (which we'll talk more about in Chapter 9, "Dow Busters").

The ways in which computers and the Internet are used are constantly changing, along with the products, services, and personnel required to support new applications. For example, we've already seen how e-commerce changed the nature of business transactions, enabling markets to expand and an increasing array of services to be provided. As the amount of computer-stored information grows, individuals, businesses, and organizations will only continue to look for ways to tap the full potential of their vast stores of data, expand their capabilities, integrate new technologies, and develop new applications, all of which leaves the IT industry poised to become one of the major employers of the new economy, providing a plethora of stable, long-term employment for workers. In the appendix, you'll find a comprehensive list of IT career resources, including certification courses, industry news, and job sites, and information on how to apply for related educational grants, scholarships, and loans.

MAKING THE TRANSITION: INFORMATION TECHNOLOGY

Kevin S., 34, of Queens, New York, works as the head of IT for a non-profit organization in New York City, but it was his quiet childhood in the Midwest that actually put him on the career path that led to working with computers. "I have always been fascinated by the future, by what it has to offer," Kevin explains. But growing up in a small farm town, he knew right away that the slower pace of life he saw there wasn't for him. His desire for a more exciting and fast-paced career path pushed Kevin toward a technical degree. "I wanted a path where I could help shape the future and have greater insight to what was occurring around me. I ended up going to grad school for math and physics and worked on a few high-level research and development projects with outside firms and institutions. As I went further along this path, it became less about the abstracts and more about the 'products,' regardless of their moral implications. This did not sit well with me, so I debated a career shift. I had always been good with computers, and at the time the world was making rock stars out of guys like Bill Gates and Steve Jobs. I thought that at the very least, folks would be hiring and that computers were a safe bet to be sticking around for the foreseeable future."

While Kevin knew a career in IT could provide long-term employment, he also knew it could offer exactly the kind of challenging position he was looking for, not to mention a profitable one. "The economics were not lost on me—the overnight Microsoft millionaires and Silicon Valley start-ups with their venture capital guardian angels—but it had more to do with me knowing that it was something that I could be good at and be entertained by. The key factor was that IT is *always* evolving. It changes and morphs every year. New tools and new practices emerge on a daily basis. The speed at which it mutates keeps things incredibly entertaining and interesting. IT was already a bit of a hobby, and my skills had gotten me to a point where I realistically thought that I could be paid for it with a bit of training or experience."

Amazingly, that training came in the form of self-education rather than formal schooling. "I've probably spent as much as two years' worth of tuition on books for myself," Kevin admits. "When I was first getting started, the Web wasn't what we think of today. Anything I wanted to learn, I had to learn from giant tomes that were $50 to $70 a pop. Today, any technical question you have can be found in seconds with a search engine or on a technical forum. I did have to play a fair amount of catch-up with those colleagues that have had formal training, but I've also found that I am a lot more flexible than they are when new ideas are introduced. I tend to pick up theory very quickly and do a decent job of making it practical. Because of this, learning a new sub skill set in IT isn't very difficult for me." However, Kevin's extensive self-training did not mean he didn't need any certification at all. "The only formal certification that I acquired is in a specific programming language/construct. I worked for a small start-up company in the early '00s, and they needed a few people to be well versed in XML. So they paid for my IBM certification, which consisted of me reading every book I could find and taking a proctored test. There was no real formal training for that, just validation that my learning methods were adequate."

Despite Kevin's enthusiasm and drive to work at the forefront of information technology, his career actually had very humble origins, with his first IT job coming about as a product of working in a retail warehouse. "I needed a part-time job and decided to work at a computer retail store, hoping for a nice employee discount so I could acquire better hardware to test my new career on," he says. "I was hired to work in the warehouse unpacking boxes, restocking shelves, painting, et cetera. It was not a good fit for me, but I did it. The parent company of the retail store was based in the same city and would regularly post job openings in the employee break room at the store locations. I noticed a programming job listed on the wall and sent in my résumé. I decided that I wanted to give programming a shot despite not having any real experience with it. I interviewed for the job, and I was just young and

arrogant enough to somehow land that job. It didn't end well, but I learned more than enough to put me on the right track and set me up for future successes—and a few failures."

When it comes to the stability of an IT career during economic downturns and job-slashing recessions, Kevin says, "I have always felt that my job is as stable as the company itself. Currently, because I am head of IT for my employer, 95 percent of the company comes across my desk at one point or another. So I felt confident that I had an accurate read on the company's position and stability within the volatile market. My fear was minimal during the worst of the recession and continues to be so today. The one time that I was a victim of an economic down-turn, the company itself did not survive—this occurred during the dot-com bust after 2001. The key thing to remember is that being laid off isn't personal 99.9 percent of the time. It is an unfortunate reality with far more contributing factors than simply forgetting to put the new cover sheet on your TPS reports or not getting along well with your supervisor."

"I am a problem solver at my core, and IT allows me the chance to do that on a daily basis," Kevin continues. While it is the new techno-logical advances and innovations in IT that keep the industry exciting and challenging for him, he admits that it takes a certain type of adven-turous worker to enter such a constantly evolving field. "Are you afraid of change? If you answer yes, do not choose this career path. It really is that simple. IT requires a certain amount of flexibility and raw deter-mination that isn't for everyone. This applies to good and bad economic times. In the good times, it's okay to look for your 'perfect company,' where the work is interesting, the atmosphere is what you would consider right for you, and the pay is what you feel is fair. Remember that you work in a business and that your employer wouldn't hesitate to fire you if it would benefit them. You should have the same attitude with your employer. During bad times, work on what you love. Create your own project. Keep this project in your back pocket at all times. If

the worst happens, you know you have something to do while hunting for work that will keep your skills sharp. And who knows? When the money starts to flow again, you may have the next Amazon or Google on your hands. There isn't one successful company out there right now that wasn't started as a pet project by at least one person who felt passionately about it."

CHAPTER 8

ENTREPRENEURSHIP

It may seem counterintuitive during a deep, painful recession when everyone's wallets are on lockdown to point to starting your own business as a viable source of income. However, I like to remind people that Bill Gates created Microsoft during the recession of the 1970s, and his little start-up went on to become the number one computer operating system and software developer in the world, doing more than $1 billion a year in revenue. Procter & Gamble began selling household products in Cincinnati, Ohio, during the Panic of 1837. FedEx started a shipping business out of Memphis International Airport in Tennessee during the oil crisis of 1973. In fact, no fewer than 16 of the 30 companies listed on the Dow Jones Industrial Average were launched during recessions. Additionally, nearly half of the 2008 Inc. 500 companies and more than half of the 2008 Fortune 500 companies were born during recessions or bear markets. So it's not just that successful new businesses can theoretically be created during a recession—they already have been and will continue to be. The current recession is no different. Even back in January 2009, when the recession was at its job-slashing worst, *Fast Company*, the magazine for and about business leaders in all industries, named self-employment/entrepreneurship one of the top jobs for 2009.

While starting your own business does often require having the money to invest in it, it doesn't mean you have to raid your 401(k) or extract your home equity. The Small Business Administration (SBA) offers loans with very attractive terms, even more so if you happen to be a veteran. The SBA can help you find a micro-loan or possibly even a small business grant. Other organizations like the Service Corps of Retired Executives (SCORE), a volunteer organization of retired business people, offer entrepreneurs free advice on how to write a business plan and get started.

It's best not to have any illusions about it. Opening your own business can be risky and takes a lot of energy. Only 80 percent of new businesses survive after the first year, a number that dwindles to 44 percent after four years, according to the SBA. Income is neither guaranteed nor necessarily steady, and you have to rely on yourself for health insurance and a retirement plan, though luckily there are some trade organizations that can help with both. Furthermore, you may not qualify for unemployment insurance benefits.

Yet going into business for yourself might also be the perfect opportunity for those tired of working for someone else but still interested in working hard. Many workers value the control self-employment gives them over their lives, and because most entrepreneurs start companies that focus on something they already enjoy, whether it's the continuation of a job they once performed for someone else or turning a lifelong hobby into a small business, it can also be far more enjoyable. A study by the American Association of Retired Persons (AARP) found that 27 percent of workers age 50 and over switch careers to become entrepreneurs and often accept a pay cut or give up pension and health-care benefits to do so. Yet 50 percent of these people report far less stress, and a remarkable 91 percent say the trade-off was worth it.

Even with our current economic woes, America remains a beacon of entrepreneurialism. In the eight years following 1996, when the dot-com boom was in its heyday, an average of 550,000 small businesses were created *every month*. In 2007, the Consortium for Entrepreneurship Education reports there were over 23,000 business start-ups *per day*. It's because of this entrepreneurial spirit that, even before the current recession, a growing number of people felt the itch to escape the desk job format and go into business for themselves, buying franchises or setting up multiple online businesses. Today, with so many out of work, a lot more people are hopping on the entrepreneurial bandwagon.

It turns out that even in a downturn, the number of business start-ups remains relatively constant—about 6 million per year. So why would people start their own businesses during such a tough economic climate? Well, believe it or not, there are actually distinct advantages to starting up during a tight economy. It allows small businesses a year or two to iron out kinks before the buying climate picks up, overhead costs tend to be lower, advertising rates are cheaper, commercial space is often easier to find, and there's less competition for talent because they can pick from a larger, more qualified pool of laid-off workers. For all these reasons, starting a business in a bad economy allows entrepreneurs to reap the positive gains as soon as the economy turns around.

When you think about it, this shouldn't be as surprising as it sounds. Entrepreneurs rarely consult the broad economic picture when trying to decide whether or not to start a business. That's because if they have a great business idea, they follow through with that idea regardless of the macro economy, just like Bill Gates did when he promised to put a computer on every desk and in every home at a time when people could barely afford their groceries. And he succeeded, too, because in

a down economy, there are vast opportunities for new ideas simply because there are more economic problems that people need solved. In Gates' case, his operating system and software wound up cutting business costs significantly enough that the state of the economy had no negative effect on his sales volume.

When credit gets crunched in a recession, you would expect to see a harder climate for entrepreneurs to get started in, and yet the lack of a significant change in the number of start-ups is a reminder of just how small a role traditional bank lending plays in starting businesses. Money from friends, family, angel investors, and small business grants and loans tend to be far more important.

Similarly, recessions turn out to be especially good times for entrepreneurs to build loyal followers. Big companies, most of which have learned the value of community building among their clientele, are distracted during a recession while they keep their heads down, reducing expenses and avoiding new investments. They are also understaffed from layoffs that have sliced whole layers out of their organizations. But when the economy recovers, they will want go after that audience once more. If an entrepreneur has already swooped in to take ownership of that audience, it gives him or her tremendous leverage in the marketplace. Launching a business during an economic crisis, therefore, can be a good time to steal market share from established but vulnerable competitors.

What's more, recessions offer entrepreneurs the most affordable brand of market research in existence. When the economy slows, customers give themselves permission to complain openly and honestly to anyone who will listen. Entrepreneurs can save themselves a great deal of money on expensive market research just by listening carefully to what customers are saying, whether it's about their own businesses or their competitors'. By paying attention to customers' needs,

entrepreneurs can focus or adjust their product or service innovations to expand their customer bases accordingly.

When it comes to entrepreneurship, innovation is key. Entrepreneurs who successfully cultivate innovation have the ability to change with the market, assess and be comfortable with risk, and balance passion and objectivity. Innovators don't just brainstorm; they test and implement ideas. They go where their target market goes and observe the needs that aren't being filled. They learn from other industries' successes *and* failures. Sound tough? It can be, but the rewards for success can also be enormous, and not just monetarily.

Triggered by the recession, an aging population, and fading job security, a perfect storm of entrepreneurship conditions is emerging right now, resulting in an unexpected opportunity for workers who have spent their professional lives making money for other people's businesses to finally invest in their own talents. Workers are taking note. Thousands of professionals stymied by the deepening recession and worsening job market are turning to starting a business as their plan B, creating a growing breed of "accidental entrepreneurs" who may never have even imagined taking the step to small business ownership until the recession handed them the opportunity.

The SBA reports that the number of small businesses is increasing in the United States, rising steadily this decade to 21.1 million in 2007, a jump from 16.5 million in 2000. Since small businesses employ fewer people than big corporations do, and sometimes have no employees at all, they have the advantage of being able to hunker down and reduce expenditures when the economy goes sour without always taking a major hit to their productivity or ability to remain competitive.

That's why Karen Mills, the head of the SBA, announced in August 2009 that it is going to be small businesses, not major corporations, that spur the economy and fuel the recovery. The

federal government would seem to agree, incorporating provisions into the Recovery Act that allow for a combination of fee reductions and higher guarantees for banks that make loans through the SBA's programs. More than 400 banks that hadn't made an SBA-backed loan since 2007 resumed lending after the Recovery Act was enacted in February 2009, and weekly loan volumes have risen 45 percent compared to the months immediately prior. There is still a ways to go when you consider that this is still 55 percent fewer loans than the SBA backed in 2007, before the recession took hold, but discussions are ongoing with the federal government about whether the SBA's loan-guarantee programs need to be expanded further, including the option to offer bigger loans. Currently, the SBA's most active program maxes out at a $2 million loan size, a limit the agency is strongly considering lifting, even if only temporarily.

The creation of new businesses, new products, and new services is absolutely critical to the stability and vibrancy of an economy. No economy can survive without the entrepreneurship necessary to create new businesses that can replace the dying ones. As business owners switch careers or retire, many businesses come to an end alongside the flow of their products and services. Unfortunately, so does the employment status of their workers. If no new start-ups replace those businesses, unemployment rises, money doesn't flow freely through the community, and the economy comes to a grinding halt. A truly vibrant economy is also characterized by the development of new products and services, including new, more efficient methods that drive out the older, less efficient methods and the outmoded businesses that use them. This way, new and more efficient products and services replace or drive out inefficient and less desirable ones, and the market progresses.

Back in 2002, when the U.S. Census Bureau conducted its most recent survey of business owners, it was reported that

self-employed individuals who have no paid employees operate three-fourths of U.S. businesses. The survey also found that small businesses represented more than 99.7 percent of the nation's total number of employers and collectively employed more than 50 percent of the private workforce. Small businesses also generated more than half of the nation's gross domestic product and were the principal source of new jobs in the U.S. economy, creating 60 percent to 80 percent of new jobs annually.

Unfortunately, the Bureau of Labor Statistics does not track data on entrepreneurs or self-employed workers of any kind, making up-to-date hard data difficult to come by, though some proposals have been put forward in recent years to find ways for the BLS to do so. Part of the problem is that the range of data is diverse and sometimes contradictory, with the collective number of small business owners rising or falling depending on what criteria is being used to count them. For example, counting the number of business openings results in a different number than counting what are called "establishment births," which are defined as the opening of brand-new businesses rather than franchises. Those numbers in turn are different from the numbers that result from counting the new Employer Identification Numbers applied for on both the state and national levels. You can see why some kind of national standard for measuring entrepreneurial activity is needed.

Luckily, until that time, we have the Kauffman Index of Entrepreneurial Activity, a report put out by the Ewing Marion Kauffman Foundation that has become the leading indicator of new business creation in the United States. The Index provides the earliest documentation of new business development across the country by capturing new business owners in their first month of significant business activity, and the results are an excellent snapshot of the entrepreneurial industry.

The Index found that in 2008, when the recession was already under way, an average of 0.32 percent of the adult population, or 320 out of every 100,000 adults, created a new business each month, representing approximately 530,000 new businesses per month—almost as many as during the dot-com boom. This is a slight increase over the 2007 rate of 0.30 percent. At the same time, from 2007 to 2008, entrepreneurship rates increased for the lowest-income-potential types of businesses, from 120 per 100,000 to 130 per 100,000, and middle-income-potential types of businesses, from 110 per 100,000 to 123 per 100,000. For the highest-income-potential types of businesses, entrepreneurship rates dipped from 73 per 100,000 to 69 per 100,000. These patterns provide convincing evidence of the difference between "necessity" and "opportunity" entrepreneurship in tough economic climates. As the creation of new low- and middle-income-potential "necessity" businesses increases—namely, start-ups that fulfill a clear community or business need—the number of new high-income-potential "opportunity" businesses, high-concept start-ups that hope to make a big splash right out of the gate through marketing, advertising, and aggressive competition, tends to decrease.

The Index is also one of the few indicators that break the entrepreneurial field down into demographic models. It found that the entrepreneurial activity rate for men increased slightly from 0.41 percent in 2007 to 0.42 percent in 2008. For women, the rate increased from 0.20 percent to 0.24 percent. The activity rate among Latinos increased from 0.40 percent in 2007 to 0.48 percent in 2008, continuing an upward Latino entrepreneurial trend that started in 2005. Asian-Americans also experienced a large increase in entrepreneurship rates, from 0.29 percent in 2007 to 0.35 percent in 2008. Non-Latino white business-creation rates increased slightly from 2007 to 2008,

from 0.30 percent to 0.31 percent, whereas African-American rates declined slightly, from 0.23 percent to 0.22 percent, possibly due to the disproportionately large effect the recession has had on African-American workers and communities (in July 2009 it had a 14.5 percent unemployment rate compared to the 9.4 percent national average for all workers). The immigrant rate of entrepreneurial activity increased from 0.46 percent in 2007 to an impressive 0.51 percent in 2008, further widening the gap between immigrant and native-born rates. Native-born rates increased only slightly, from 0.27 percent to 0.28 percent. The increase in entrepreneurship rates from 2007 to 2008 among immigrants was driven entirely by low- and medium-income-potential types of businesses, the Index found. However, immigrants were also found to be more likely to start high-income-potential types of businesses than the native born.

The Index also discovered that while business creation rates increased for less-educated individuals, the college-educated experienced a decline in entrepreneurial activity rates, from 0.33 percent in 2007 to 0.31 percent in 2008. The oldest age group, ages 55 to 64, experienced the largest increase in entrepreneurial activity from 2007 to 2008, from 0.31 percent to 0.36 percent, making it the age group with the highest entrepreneurial activity rate due to the amount of workers who begin second careers as entrepreneurs after retiring, often having both the experience and the savings to make a go of it. The number of older entrepreneurs is likely to climb as well because long-term employment has fallen for those between 35 and 64, the Index suggests. Furthermore, Americans in general are living longer than ever before, giving workers more years after a late-career layoff or early retirement to start a new business.

The construction industry was found to have the highest entrepreneurial activity rate of all major industry groups in 2008

at 1.38 percent, despite the fact that construction work was hit hard by the recession. The second-highest entrepreneurial activity rate was in the services industry at 0.41 percent. Entrepreneurship increased in all regions of the United States from 2007 to 2008, except in the Midwest. There, the business creation rate declined slightly from 0.25 percent to 0.23 percent, possibly due to how hard the Midwest-based manufacturing industry was pummeled by the recession. The states with the highest entrepreneurial activity rates were found to be Georgia, with 590 entrepreneurs per 100,000 adults; New Mexico, with 580 per 100,000; Montana, with 530 per 100,000; Arizona, with 490 per 100,000; Alaska, with 440 per 100,000; and California, with 440 per 100,000. The states with the lowest entrepreneurial activity rates were Pennsylvania, with only 140 per 100,000 adults; Missouri, with 150 per 100,000; Wisconsin, with 170 per 100,000; West Virginia, with 170 per 100,000; Iowa, with 190 per 100,000 adults; and Ohio, with 190 per 100,000.

The states experiencing the largest increases in entrepreneurial activity rates over the past decade, according to the Index, were Georgia, with a 0.17 percent increase, Mississippi with 0.12 percent, Massachusetts with 0.09 percent, New York with 0.09 percent, and Rhode Island with 0.08 percent. The states that experienced the largest decreases in their rates were Alaska, down by 0.23 percent, North Dakota by 0.19 percent, New Mexico by 0.18 percent, and Iowa by 0.13 percent.

The first thing for an entrepreneur to do when considering business prospects for tough economic times is to think of what needs may emerge. Recessions mean extensive unemployment, difficulty in personal and company bill paying, a decrease in sales of products and services, home and business foreclosures, and a businesswide trend in cutting operating and capital costs. Unemployed workers need assistance in finding new jobs, so a lot of entrepreneurs are taking advantage of the

opportunity by starting employment agencies, life coaching services, personal image consulting, job skills training, or résumé writing, making money while also performing a valuable public service. (The intrinsic joy of matching unemployed workers with employers cannot be overstated. It's one of the reasons I wrote this book.)

Aside from helping workers find jobs, another top prospect for small businesses continues to be Internet companies. That's because over the past five years, as broadband Internet connections became as commonplace as indoor plumbing, the model for launching a Web company has changed. In the old days, Internet start-ups tended to get funded before they launched. Entrepreneurs first put their energy into writing business plans to attract investors, and then only after the money was in hand did they get down to work. But there were a couple of drawbacks to using this otherwise sound model for Web companies. First, entrepreneurs frequently ended up owning only a tiny percentage of their own companies as their ownership became further diluted each time they brought in new rounds of investments. Second, it turned out there was often no true correlation between the assumptions put forth in a theoretical business plan and the reality of Internet businesses. Many great business plans turned into lousy start-ups, which was one of the primary reasons for the dot-com crash.

But these days, especially with the recession, Internet start-ups are increasingly following the LILO formula—that is, "a little in, a lot out." These Web-based businesses cost almost nothing to get off the ground, yet can turn into great money-makers through hard work and patience. With LILOs, the old business plan formula takes a back seat to trying the idea first at minimal expense, without having to persuade others to buy in. That's because the amount of time and money spent mapping out the business and attempting to lure investors is now

almost higher than the cost of simply trying it. Often, these LILO companies can get off the ground for the cost of a domain name, a programmer, and a Web site designer.

A bad economy can be the LILO Internet business's friend. The cost of failure is cheap compared to, say, starting up and closing down a brick-and-mortar retail establishment, so entrepreneurs find they can afford numerous times at bat without breaking the bank. This also creates a better environment for risk-taking, which is the only way innovation occurs. Similarly, launching in a bad economy can impose valuable lessons in discipline on a business owner, forcing entrepreneurs to keep costs low and make smart decisions about marketing and distribution.

Bizstarters.com, which offers coaching to new start-ups, advises entrepreneurs, especially older ones, to launch businesses from their homes and rely on independent contractors instead of employees in order to keep costs down. With technology costs lower than ever, many people are starting businesses for just a few hundred dollars a month in expenses, greatly reducing the financial risk. With annual expenses closer to $6,000 than $60,000 or more, the risk quotient goes way down, making this approach an attractive one for entrepreneurs worried about how they're going to keep their heads above water during the often difficult starting months.

Right now also happens to be a great time to start a repair business. When money is tight and people are out of work, they tend to keep their items for longer, so the demand for everyday repair work remains steady. In some cases, the demand even grows. The average auto body shop, for example, is getting customers who would rather keep their old cars for a few more years instead of buying new ones. But the existing businesses aren't hiring more people to cover that demand, and as a result, they're turning customers away, creating a palpable need for

better service throughout communities all over the country. A smart entrepreneur can fill that need and, at the same time, create a loyal, grateful customer base for the life of the business. That life could be a pretty long one, too. The job of fixing someone's roof, car, or refrigerator is in no danger of being outsourced to China.

Small businesses like these that fill an existing need are what get money flowing again in a local economy, and eventually in the national economy as a whole. That's what Karen Mills meant when she said small businesses will spur the economic recovery. All it takes is someone with the courage to start a business that fills a need. The demand is there, and it is those who meet this demand who will come out on top when the economy fully recovers.

Business opportunities for entrepreneurs are limitless, even during a recession. The economic downturn is no reason not to explore new business ventures. In fact, for entrepreneurs, the recession is leveling the playing field. Big businesses suffer in a bad economy because of high overhead costs, and as these overstuffed businesses lose market share or disappear altogether, new opportunities emerge for small businesses to pick up the slack. The moneymaking ideas might be different from those that exist during economic boom times, but I can assure you the resulting cash flow spends just as well.

Plus, it never hurts to mention that the vast majority of the nation's millionaires are entrepreneurs.

Consulting

Money is tight for everyone right now, so your own finances may tell you it's not necessarily be the greatest time to open a McDonald's franchise or that vintage auto restoration shop

you've always dreamed of owning. Luckily, there is another self-employment option that doesn't require a big cash outlay or any of the financial risks of opening a new business: consulting, where workers can hire themselves out to employers on a per-project basis, and the start-up cost is often just new business cards and a Web presence.

Just because employers can't afford to keep workers on staff anymore doesn't mean they don't still have need of their expertise. During economic downturns, many laid-off workers keep the income rolling in by hiring themselves out as freelance consultants, sometimes even to the same companies that were forced to lay them off as full-time employees.

In fact, since the recession began, freelance professionals now make up more than a quarter of the nation's working population, or 26 percent, according to a survey by human resources consulting firm Kelly Services, Inc. That's up from 19 percent in 2006.

With unemployment numbers at record highs and businesses constricting in order to stay afloat, there are more people than ever looking for new ways to earn money, but there are also more companies looking to make fulfilling their talent needs more cost-efficient. Freelancing kills two birds with one stone. For businesses, taking advantage of freelance labor saves money. They can hire contract workers instead of full-time employees and thus only pay for workers when they need them, allowing employers to hire personnel for short-term projects without having to make long-term commitments. This also saves employers money by cutting back on costly benefit packages. For cost-conscious businesses, these factors make hiring contract workers an attractive prospect.

However, the risks are similar to those of small business entrepreneurs. Paychecks can be erratic. Contract workers are

vulnerable during down times, often the first ones let go when companies decide to scale back. Moreover, the self-employed have to pay out of pocket for their own health insurance, have to fund their own retirement plans, and generally do not qualify for unemployment insurance benefits. Still, like small business owners, many consultants enjoy the freedom and control that freelancing gives them over their careers and consider the trade-off to be a good one—especially in this day and age when even in robust economic times there is no guarantee that a job will be around forever. Rather than leaving their employment fates in someone else's hands, independent consultants find it much more satisfying to take charge of their own careers and their own futures.

Many workers move into consulting after gaining experience in their particular fields through years of traditional employment. As a result, the average age in the consulting industry is higher than in most others, while the proportion of younger workers is lower:

- Ages 16 to 19 finds 0.2 percent employment in consulting, compared to 4.3 percent in other industries
- Ages 20 to 24 finds 4.4 percent in consulting, compared to 9.6 percent in other industries
- Ages 25 to 34 finds 19.8 percent in consulting, compared to 21.5 percent in other industries
- Ages 35 to 44 finds 24.7 percent in consulting, compared to 23.9 percent in other industries
- Ages 45 to 54 finds 24.7 percent in consulting, compared to 23.6 percent in other industries
- Ages 55 to 64 finds 18.9 percent in consulting, compared to 13.4 percent in other industries
- Ages 65 and older finds 7.1 percent in consulting, compared to 3.7 percent in other industries

As mentioned in Chapter 7, although a consultant's qualifications are important, they are not necessarily the only deciding factor for companies looking to contract with one. Just as important is the consultant's approach. Employers want consultants who can listen to their needs and come up with quick, practical solutions. So it's not just how much a consultant knows, but he or she applies that knowledge. Consultants must also develop the practical skills needed to run their own businesses, as well as identifying the best advisors in areas such as accounting, taxation, and legal issues. As mentioned earlier, it's not for everyone, but for those who have the self-discipline, motivation, and determination to take on the unpredictable world of freelance, it can be a very successful career shift.

A recent article in *Consultant Journal* calls consulting in a recession a veritable ticket to success. Hyperbole aside, the article has a valid point, going on to list a number of ways that a recession can help, rather than hinder, those in the consulting field. For example:

- Fears of a downturn can send competitors heading for the hills, making more opportunities available.
- Businesses inevitably look to cut costs during a recession and will outsource more work to independent contractors.
- Businesses worry about expensive, long-term commitments during a recession and instead turn to hiring consultants to get projects done rather than taking on permanent employees.
- Businesses know that they're going to have to work harder to keep their clients happy, and after massive layoffs have gutted their departments, they will need the specialized expertise of consultants in order to remain competitive.

- Independent consultants tend to cost less than consultants leased out from big consulting firms, and therefore, they have a competitive advantage during recessions over consulting firms with higher costs, long-term leases, and other commitments.
- During a recession, the strength of the U.S dollar weakens, making it easier to pick up clients in Canada, the United Kingdom, and other countries that have stronger currencies.
- Workers running an independent consulting business during a recession quickly learn how to hone their business management skills, making them stronger and more attractive workers in the long run.

For these reasons, there is probably no better time to be out there selling professional services as a consultant. As companies continue to shift their focus from growth to cost reduction, contracting for necessary talent will only increase. The bottom line is that consultants provide businesses with access to specialized labor and abilities at the reduced price that businesses are looking for during these tough times. As local service providers, consultants have never been in a better position to take advantage of this dramatic shift in the marketplace.

Look at it this way. Every department or function within a business requires a group of skill sets. Some workers are good at one or two of these, but no one is good at all of them. This means companies are forced to hire more people than they need in order to cover all the skills necessary. The result is a workforce of underutilized employees. Ultimately, these over-staffed businesses are forced to scale back during a recession and lay off workers, but the functions are still there, with demands that still need to be met, and that leaves employers with a difficult choice. They can either force their remaining workers to stretch into areas where they have no experience or

expertise, resulting in increased human error and decreased efficiency, or they can reach out to consultants and get exactly the skills they require, at exactly the time that they are required.

The ventures that manage to do well in tough economic times are often the ones that are flexible and creative, and self-employed consultants have much more freedom in that respect. Provided, of course, they have the reputation, track record. and contacts to find clients. Finding work as a consultant is all about playing to your strengths and networking. Contract work often comes through referrals and word of mouth. Therefore, consultants frequently have to reach out to a variety of sources in order to find opportunities, such as school alumni contacts that work in the industry or at firms that may have need of consultants, family and friends, and former work colleagues who work in consulting themselves or are well connected. The more people consultants tell their goals to, the better chance they will have of being referred to human resources contacts, other consultants, and consulting firms.

In terms of overall job growth, one of the nation's fastest-growing industries is niche business consulting, with a cumulative workforce that is expected to increase by 5.9 percent through 2016. Corporate layoffs have spawned a wave of professionals who are trying to repurpose their skills in the consulting realm. While the competition is fierce in this arena, the barriers to entry are low, and the industry as a whole is seeing a shift as clients drop big corporate consultancies in favor of independent contractors and smaller, more specialized firms. Particularly in demand right now, for obvious reasons, are consultants who can help companies to save money and minimize financial losses.

As mentioned in the previous chapter, one of the most in-demand niches right now is IT consulting. Our society runs on technology, and technology runs much of our lives. From PCs

to cell phones to networks, people rely on systems they don't really understand. Businesses are much the same way. They need the expertise of an IT professional to make the pieces work together regardless of whether they can afford to keep IT workers on permanent staff, which is why computer systems analyst consultants are projected to enjoy 29 percent employment growth by 2016. Furthermore, there are more outside threats to confidential, protected data now than ever before. Businesses, especially small businesses, have data they need to protect, but they don't know how. IT security consultants are finding a thriving livelihood in helping companies figure out what they need to protect and how best to protect it, and as a result, they are projected to see 27 percent job growth by 2016.

IT consulting also meets the current demand for consultants who can save businesses money and minimize financial loss. IBM recently reported that despite the pressure to cut costs, businesses are proceeding with IT plans that range from information management to social media and cloud computing, all involving specialized, cutting-edge technology that requires consultants with the expertise to create, implement, and instruct the company on how to use those technologies. The IBM report went on to identify the top five trends for companies that point to how in demand IT consulting is during the recession and beyond:

- The highest-priority technology solution, chosen by 75 percent of the businesses polled, is information management, which turns mountains of data into meaningful insights.
- When asked to list their most pressing business challenges, 80 percent included increasing efficiency and productivity, 74 percent included improving customer care, and 72 percent included the better use of information.

- The impact of the economy on IT budgets has caused 53 percent of businesses to actually increase or reprioritize their spending, with only 37 percent reporting a decrease.
- Despite the economy, more than two-thirds of those businesses surveyed are planning to implement or are currently implementing their top IT priorities.
- A majority of firms view their primary IT provider as a technology advisor or IT and business consultant, with 25 percent seeing the relationship as purely transactional.

Another high-demand niche are green consultants, who help companies analyze their current or planned environment and find ways to make it more sustainable and environmentally friendly. Green consultants are experts in one or more areas dealing with ecology and sustainability, and specialize in everything from green architecture and design to green consumerism. Wherever there is a need, green consultants guide their clients toward a more sustainable existence.

In the coming years, green consultants will be in higher demand than ever before, with a projected job growth of 25 percent by 2016. People are increasingly more aware of their natural environment, the dangers of global warming, and expensive, wasteful energy habits, and businesses are following suit, especially now with the Obama administration's commitment to green energy and infrastructure. As the green economy heats up, more businesses are looking to go green, fully aware that being environmentally friendly is becoming increasingly important to their customers and prospective customers. They also do not want to suffer the possibly disastrous fate of being held up in the media as an environmental polluter. However, these companies often have no clue where to start or how to do so and save money at the same time, leading them to hire green consultants to save them the time and resources

they would otherwise have to invest in learning how to make the necessary changes on their own.

The list of environmentally responsible movements and efforts by business is significant and growing, including energy conservation efforts, water quality preservation, alternative energy projects, employee carpool encouragement, community cleanups, land reclamation, recycling, Green Star energy compliance, and more. This leaves the door wide open for workers looking to plug themselves into this growing field as green consultants and show businesses how to become more energy-efficient and save money at the same time.

Small businesses that want to go green often have a tougher time of it than big corporations, which have more financial resources at their disposal. The average small business owner is not likely to be up on the ways to save energy, conserve water, or decrease chemical utilization. Most small business owners also may not know how to fully take advantage of the potentially positive public relations aspect of going green that can bring in more customers, nor are they likely to have the resources to hire a staff member to take on these tasks, putting them in desperate need of a green consultant's expertise and guidance.

One type of consultant that is always in demand is the management consultant. Businesses are continually faced with new challenges, especially during difficult times, and as a result, they increasingly rely on management consultants, also known as management analysts, to analyze and propose ways to improve an organization's structure, efficiency, or profits and help them remain competitive amidst a changing economic climate. Some management consultants specialize in a specific industry, such as health care or telecommunications, while others specialize by type of business function, such as human resources, marketing, logistics, or information systems.

Management consultants also find numerous government opportunities, where they tend to specialize by type of agency. Currently, we see management consultants that specialize in specific high-growth areas like biotechnology, health care, information technology, human resources, engineering, and marketing is in especially high demand right now.

Both public and private organizations use management consultants for a variety of reasons. For instance, a company might lack the internal resources needed to handle a project, or it might need a management consultant's expertise to determine what resources will be required and what problems may be encountered if they pursue a particular opportunity. Management consultants exist to increase efficiency and worker productivity, and to control costs.

There are currently about 678,000 management consultants in the United States, and 27 percent of them are self-employed. That's three times the average of self-employment in other occupations. The number of management consultants is expected to grow by 22 percent by 2016, adding another 149,000 consultants to the field.

This growth is being driven by an increasing industry and government reliance on outside expertise to improve the performance of their organizations. A number of changes in the business environment have forced companies to take a closer look at their operations. It's not just the economy, either. These changes include new business regulations, developments in IT, and the expansion of electronic commerce.

The growth of international business has also contributed to an increase in demand for management consultants. Many businesses expanding abroad hire management consultants to help them form the right strategy for entering the market, to advise them on legal matters pertaining to specific countries, and to help them with organizational, administrative, and

other issues, especially if the U.S. company is involved in a partnership or merger with a foreign one.

International and domestic markets have become more competitive in recent years, and businesses need to use resources more efficiently, resulting in a progressing increase in management consultants being sought to help reduce costs, streamline operations, and develop marketing strategies. With businesses downsizing to remain competitive in a down market, we can expect to see more opportunities created for management consultants to perform duties that used to be handled internally. Of course, the public sector needs management analysts, too, with federal, state, and local government agencies looking for ways to become more efficient.

For some, independent consulting can also be the perfect intermediate step between self-employment and regaining full-time employment. If a business that hires a consultant for an individual project is impressed by that consultant's abilities and likes working with him or her, it might offer a permanent position in the company. Independent consultants can also sometimes be recruited by consulting firms, where they can continue as per-project workers while reclaiming the stability of a steady paycheck.

American entrepreneurship is as old as the nation itself. Our do-it-yourself spirit—"me-preneurship," if you will—is one of the core business principles that set the United States apart from other countries. As you saw in this chapter, entrepreneurship, whether it's opening a small business or becoming self-employed as an independent consultant, doesn't stop in a tough job market or down economy. Quite the opposite, it heats up.

Many workers are taking advantage of the current recession to start their own businesses, steal market share from vulnerable competitors, and hire the best and brightest of the recession's

"brain drain" to staff their start-ups, leaving them in an advantageous position when the economy finally recovers. Others, like 26 percent of the nation's current working population, are finding their way back into the black through self-employment as consultants, taking advantage of the fact that businesses still have a need for their expertise even if they can't afford to hire them as permanent employees. A down job market is the perfect time for workers who have always dreamed of owning their own business or who can handle the freelance lifestyle to go into business for themselves. In the appendix, you'll find a comprehensive list of career resources for entrepreneurs and consultants, including industry news, freelance and recruitment job sites, and information on how to apply for small business loans, grants, and investments.

MAKING THE TRANSITION: ENTREPRENEURSHIP

Dan W., 35, of Lexington, Kentucky, already had a background in retail before he decided to open his own video rental store in the thriving Carroll Gardens neighborhood of Brooklyn, New York, in 2002. In college he studied studio arts, which he says was "never directly relevant in any job I've ever held. I had all manner of retail jobs while in college, including a couple of years at an indie record store. Out of college, in San Francisco, I worked as the music buyer in a small new-age shop—music was a small part of their operation . . . incense, new age books, jewelry, that kind of stuff—and then Amoeba Music. Amoeba was probably my biggest inspiration in terms of how to run my own store. Though it was huge, a former bowling alley, it still had the feel of an indie mom-and-pop. Knowledgeable without being pretentious. They also treated their staff very well and kept us happy and interested in our jobs."

After that, Dan moved into Web jobs. "It was the Bay Area dot-com gold rush of the late '90s, and I had writing and editing gigs for two major Web sites. One was an entertainment-based site, and the other was the Web site for a major city newspaper."

But Dan's interest in retail never dissipated and quickly returned to the fore when he realized that working for someone else was not necessarily the key to job security. "Having lived through the boom and bust of the dot-com scene on the West Coast, I figured getting laid off, which I avoided twice and didn't once, was no more or less hazardous than opening my own business." He had always been a big fan of movies and video stores, so that was where his mind turned when he first considered becoming an entrepreneur. "In San Francisco, which has quite a number of great stores, the thought of opening my own never crossed my mind," he explains. But he soon discovered New York City was a different creature altogether when he moved to the borough of Brooklyn in 2002. "In Brooklyn, there were only three kinds of video stores: indie but obnoxious, mom-and-pop but clueless, and the corporate giants like Blockbuster. I went from 'I could open a better video store' to 'I *could* open a better video store!'"

However, it took a few months of living and working in New York before he was ready to make the transition from working for someone else to going into business for himself. "When I arrived, I had a single job lead, from a friend I'd grown up with, and that single interview landed me the job as an associate producer/editor with an entertainment search site from a major global Internet service company. It was actually a step down from my previous job. My job in San Francisco as an entertainment editor was actually interesting and challenging. We had to pick and choose articles to put on the Web site, write snappy headlines, write and edit guides and reviews of all sorts." Finding his new job far less exciting, it was this sense of being unfulfilled and unchallenged that energized Dan's entrepreneurial spirit. "As soon as I started this new job, the video store idea germinated, and I coasted through my six

months on the job while doing research and legwork for the store, before quitting in September '02 to work full-time on the business."

Dan didn't take the traditional route to funding his new business venture, choosing to eschew SBA loans and private lending companies in favor of a small loan from his mother. "It just seemed like the easiest and most obvious answer," he explains of his decision to keep it in the family. It freed him from having to adhere to the more strict repayment timeline of a small business loan. "Being a very unofficial kind of loan, I've been paying her back on and off for years now."

Ultimately, his business became so successful that it not only outlasted its neighboring competitors, but it also allowed Dan to move back to his hometown of Lexington, Kentucky, with his wife and daughter in 2007 and live off the store's income, leaving the day-to-day operations in the hands of his manager and staff. While he admits that the recession has put a dent in his video rental business, it's only a small one. "Our sales had been going up steadily since we opened in fall of 2002. But starting in the early fall of 2008, we experienced our first decline, not coincidentally at the beginning of the bank failures. We've been down, but not terribly so, since then. I'm not too worried about it, but I'm hoping for a good winter season, which is traditionally our best time of the year."

When asked if he feels more fulfilled in his career after becoming an entrepreneur, Dan replies, "Absolutely. I was an associate production manager at one of my early Web jobs, but I still couldn't tell you what exactly we did there. It was a major business entity trying to get into the search engine game, and ultimately it went nowhere. But seriously, I had no idea what we were trying to accomplish. I would walk out of meetings shrugging. It was a serious breath of fresh air to make a brick-and-mortar store where you, philosophically, buy something for one dollar and sell it for two. I can't imagine working for anyone else at this point."

He also has some advice for other people looking to open their own businesses. "There are two elements that you have to be good at: the

'thing' that you're selling—shoes, videos, yoga lessons—and the business itself. You have to budget for expenses beyond the grand opening. Forget about being all things to all people or fighting off larger competitors. Just do one thing and do it well."

CHAPTER 9

DOW BUSTERS

E ven when the market craters and millions find themselves out of work, there are a handful of jobs that seem to be recession-proof, careers that remain in demand—and in a few cases, grow in demand—while cutbacks and layoffs affect everyone else. Some of the fields highlighted in this chapter are traditionally recession-proof, continuing to grow and hire no matter how far the Dow drops, while others are examples of occupations that are weathering the storm during the current recession due to the particular services they offer.

Accounting

As you might imagine, recruitment in the accounting industry is at its busiest around tax season, but the overall hiring of accountants has remained steady even while other occupations face cutbacks and layoffs. The reason is that employers rely on accountants to manage their financial systems, file their taxes, and handle other tasks that are imperative to their business no matter what shape the economy is in. In fact, accounting is one of those rare occupations that seems to thrive during recessions. Companies trying to cut costs and not overspend put

more importance on the good financial controls that require accountants, especially those who perform internal audits, credit collection, and operations analysis. With financial firms under intense scrutiny and new regulations currently being discussed, we're likely to see an increase in auditing firms, creating thousands of new jobs for accountants.

Accountants hold over 1 million jobs throughout private industry and government, though 21 percent of the workforce are employed by accounting, tax preparation, bookkeeping, and payroll firms, while 10 percent are self-employed. Some 3,500 new accounting positions were created in March and April of 2009, and employment is projected to grow 15 percent *annually* for the next decade. Additionally, this is an aging profession that the industry estimates will lose 75 percent of its current employees to retirement by 2020, which means job openings will be abundant for years. Accountants tend to have superior job security, pay, and mobility, with opportunities to progress up the management ladder, open up a small consultancy, or do contract work. An accountant's skill set is easily transferable across regions and industries as well, giving accountants the luxury of being able to comfortably go wherever the jobs are in any economic climate.

Individuals who are proficient in accounting computer software, or have expertise in specialized areas like international business, specific industries, or current legislation, will likely have an added advantage in landing accounting jobs.

Customer Service

In an increasingly technological world, there will always be a place for customer service reps to help guide people through the tech maze, but the national rise of the service industry as a

whole is creating even greater demand for customer service reps to interact with the customers who have purchased, or are interested in purchasing, a company's products or services. That's why the occupation is expected to grow by 25 percent by 2016, adding 545,000 new jobs to the already 2.2 million workers employed in this field.

Although customer service reps are found in a wide variety of industries, about 23 percent of them work in finance and insurance, with the largest numbers employed by insurance carriers, insurance agencies and brokerages, and banks and credit unions. About 14 percent are employed in administrative and support services, the majority of which are concentrated in business support, such as banks and credit card companies, and employment services, such as temporary help services and employment placement agencies. Another 11 percent of customer service reps are employed in retail trade establishments like general merchandise stores and food and beverage stores. Other industries that employ significant numbers of customer service reps include telecommunications, manufacturing, wholesale trade, and hospitality.

Beyond growth stemming from the expansion of the industries in which customer service representatives are employed, a need for additional workers is likely to result from heightened reliance on these employees. Customer service is crucial to the success of any business or organization that deals with customers, and strong customer service builds sales, visibility, and loyalty as companies try to distinguish themselves from their competitors. For many industries, gaining a competitive edge and retaining customers will be increasingly important over the next decade, particularly in financial services, communications, and utilities. Even better, the customer service occupation generally tends to be resistant to major fluctuations in employment during recessions.

Dental Hygiene

You know those folks who work with your dentist by scraping your teeth during cleanings or giving you anesthetics when you need to have a tooth pulled? Well, believe it or not, dental hygienists are not only in constant demand, they currently rank among the fastest growing occupations in the country. There are about 167,000 dental hygienists employed in the United States, almost all of whom are employed in offices of dentists, while a very small number work for employment services, offices of physicians, or other industries. With a projected 30 percent employment increase by the year 2016, adding 50,000 new jobs to the field, dental hygiene is an unexpected but attractive source of job security.

As the need for dental care expands due to population growth, older people are increasingly retaining more teeth, and a growing focus on preventative dental care, dentists are relying more heavily on dental hygienists for cleaning, X rays, and preventative care so that they can devote their time to more complex procedures. What's more, as a large number of older dentists who have been traditionally less likely to employ dental hygienists retire from the industry, they will be replaced by recent dental school graduates who are more likely to employ hygienists to help handle the workload.

Engineering

You've probably already noticed the widespread application of engineering in the growth industries covered in this book. For example, industrial engineers are expected to grow by an amazing 53.1 percent in the biotech industry, and that's just one sector of the rapidly growing engineering field as a whole.

Engineers remain in high demand because companies still need people to design their products, whether those products are medical supplies, pharmaceutical drugs, green energy infrastructure, computers, defense weapons, or just new roads and bridges. With the manufacturing industry hurting during the recession, they're looking for ways to become more efficient and hiring technical and industrial engineers to help them. More engineering jobs are likely to open up thanks to the Obama administration's focus on using Recovery Act funds to improve infrastructure.

Engineering currently employs about 1.5 million workers, 37 percent of which are found in manufacturing industries, and another 28 percent in the professional, scientific, and technical services sector—primarily in architectural engineering. Federal, state, and local governments employ 12 percent of engineers, mainly in the U.S. Departments of Defense, Transportation, Agriculture, Interior, and Energy, as well as in NASA. Most engineers in state and local government agencies work in the highways and public works departments. About 3 percent of engineers are self-employed, many as consultants. The remaining 20 percent tend to be spread out through the construction, telecommunications, and wholesale trade industries.

Engineering as an industry is expected to see 11 percent employment growth by 2016, but if you break down the field into its component specialties, you'll see some even more impressive growth numbers by individual occupation:

- Environmental engineers are expected to grow by 25 percent
- Biomedical engineers by 21 percent
- Industrial engineers by 20 percent
- Civil engineers by 18 percent
- Marine engineers by 11 percent

- Aerospace engineers by 10 percent
- Health and safety engineers by 10 percent
- Mining and geological engineers by 10 percent
- Agricultural engineers by 9 percent
- Chemical engineers by 8 percent
- Nuclear engineers by 7 percent
- Electrical engineers by 6 percent
- General engineers by 6 percent
- Computer hardware engineers by 5 percent
- Petroleum engineers by 5 percent
- Mechanical engineers by 4 percent
- Electronics engineers by 4 percent
- Materials engineers by 4 percent

Environmental engineers are experiencing the fastest growth at 25 percent, while civil engineers are seeing the largest employment increase, with an estimated 46,000 new jobs by 2016. Not surprising when you consider that developing solutions to environmental problems and designing and supervising the construction of roads, buildings, airports, tunnels, dams, bridges, and water supply and sewage systems are major components of two of the Obama administration's main areas of focus for Recovery Act spending: green energy and infrastructure upgrades.

Even in slower growing or declining manufacturing industries, engineers are still needed to design, build, test, and improve products, but it's the faster growing service industries that are generating most of the employment growth. Competitive pressures and advancing technology is forcing companies to improve and update their product designs and optimize their manufacturing processes, making employers even more reliant on engineers to increase productivity and expand output of goods and services. With new technologies continuing to

improve the design process, engineers can produce and analyze various product designs much faster than ever before. However, unlike in some other occupations, technological advances are not expected to limit employment opportunities in engineering, because engineers will continue to develop new products and processes that increase productivity. Even with the threat of out-sourcing American engineering jobs to cheaper foreign firms, there will always be a need for on-site engineers to interact with supervisors, other employees, and clients.

Finance

I know what you're thinking: "Joe, you're crazy; you just said in Chapter 5 that 100,000 workers are estimated to lose jobs in the financial sector by the second quarter of 2010." True, but a gloomy economy leads to more people searching for safe places to put their money, and that is the bread and butter of the personal financial advisor, turning their field into a reces-sion-proof one. Consider this: We've got 77 million baby boomers who are getting ready to retire and will need help managing their money. As the economy slowly recovers and the financial industry rebounds (because it always does), the retirement of the baby boomer workforce will mean expanded job opportunities for personal financial advisors, as well as their corporate cousins, financial analysts. In fact, the BLS has forecast that personal financial advisors will be one of the 10 fastest growing occupations in the nation.

There are currently about 221,000 financial analyst jobs in the United States and 176,000 personal financial advisor jobs. More than two out of five financial analysts work in the finance and insurance industries, including securities and commodity brokers, banks and credit institutions, and insurance carriers,

while others work throughout private industry and government. Much like financial analysts, more than half of personal financial advisors work in finance and insurance industries, including securities and commodity brokers, banks, insurance carriers, and financial investment firms. However, about 30 percent of personal financial advisors are self-employed, operating small investment advisory firms.

By 2016, employment of personal finance advisors is expected to grow by an amazing 41 percent, adding 72,000 jobs to the field. Financial analyst employment is expected to grow by 34 percent, adding 75,000 jobs.

It's not only the retiring baby boomers that are keeping personal financial advisors afloat. Many companies have replaced traditional pension plans with retirement savings programs, which means more workers are managing their own retirements than in the past. In addition, people are living longer and need to plan for longer retirements.

For financial analysts, the increasing complexity of investments and the new financial regulations currently being discussed are also stimulating growth as more people are needed to analyze opportunities in the new economy and navigate the regulation maze. Additionally, because mutual funds tend to do better in a tough market than individual stocks, the number and type of mutual funds and the amount of assets invested in them should spur a demand in mutual fund companies for more financial analysts to research and recommend investments.

Firefighting

As with police officers mentioned in Chapter 6, there's always room for more firefighters. Total employment in the firefighting service is about 361,000 workers, with about 9 out of 10

firefighting workers employed by local government. Most of the remainder work in fire departments on federal and state installations, including airports, while private firefighting companies employ a small number.

Firefighters compose 293,000 workers in the service, supervisors/managers of firefighters compose about 52,000 workers and fire inspectors and investigators compose about 14,000 workers. Note, though, that these figures do not cover the hundreds of thousands of volunteer firefighters across the nation who perform the same duties and may constitute the majority of firefighters in some residential areas. Still, an overall growth projection of 12 percent means an additional 43,000 paid jobs in firefighting by the year 2016.

The firefighting service is made up of a number of roles, each with its own projected growth:

- Firefighters are expected to grow by 12 percent, adding 328,000 new jobs to the field.
- Supervisors/managers of firefighting and prevention workers by 11 percent, adding 6,000 new jobs.
- Fire inspectors and investigators by 11 percent, adding 1,500 new jobs.
- Forest fire inspectors and prevention specialists by 2 percent, adding 100 new jobs.

It's a dangerous job, definitely one that is a calling for most of the workers it employs. Still, many people are attracted to firefighting for reasons beyond the challenge and opportunity to perform an essential public service. Chief among the benefits of a job in firefighting is a pension that's usually guaranteed after 25 years in the service. Consequently, there's some keen competition out there for each job opening. However, when areas develop and become more densely populated,

emergencies and fires affect more buildings and more people, and a trend toward more people living in and around cities is increasing the demand for firefighters nationwide.

Insurance

The insurance industry remains reliable through hard times because it's not a discretionary purchase. People are always in need of coverage in case of natural disasters, theft, and health-care expenses. Some insurance purchases are even mandatory. For example, all 50 states have laws that require, or at the very least strongly recommend, that the owners and operators of automobiles have insurance.

Many insurance companies will assist recruits in obtaining the necessary licenses and certifications to become underwriters, actuaries, and claims adjusters. What's more, insurance companies hire people with diverse backgrounds and all levels of experience. Many jobs in the insurance industry use skills that are prevalent in fields like corporate finance, law, and customer service, which makes a career switch to insurance even more feasible.

The insurance industry currently employs over 2 million workers, and those numbers are expected to grow by 7.4 percent by 2016. Insurance carriers, the large companies that provide insurance and assume the risks covered by the policy, account for 62 percent of insurance jobs, while insurance agencies and brokerages, which sell insurance policies for the carriers either independently or through direct affiliation, account for 38 percent of the jobs.

Believe it or not, it's not insurance agents who make the majority of jobs in this industry; it's office and administrative

support roles at 43.6 percent of employment. These roles include the following:

- Customer service representatives, who compose 11.5 percent of all workers in the industry
- Insurance claims and policy processing clerks, who compose 9.6 percent
- Office clerks, who compose 4.6 percent
- Supervisors/managers of office and administrative support workers, who compose 2.7 percent
- Secretaries, who compose 2.7 percent
- Executive secretaries and administrative assistants, who compose 2.4 percent
- Bookkeeping, accounting and auditing clerks, who compose 2 percent
- Receptionists and information clerks, who compose 1 percent
- Data entry keyers, who compose 0.9 percent
- Billing and posting clerks and machine operators, who compose 0.8 percent
- File clerks, who compose 0.7 percent
- Mail clerks and mail machine operators, who compose 0.6 percent

Management, business, and financial occupations make up 28.6 percent of employment. These include the following:

- Claims adjusters, examiners, and investigators, who compose 9.4 percent of all workers
- Insurance underwriters, who compose 3.9 percent
- General and operations managers, who compose 1.8 percent

- Accountants and auditors, who compose 1.7 percent
- Human resources, training, and labor relations specialists, who compose 1.2 percent
- Management analysts, who compose 1.2 percent
- Financial managers, who compose 1 percent
- Marketing and sales managers, who compose 0.9 percent
- Financial analysts, who compose 0.7 percent
- Computer and information systems managers, who compose 0.6 percent
- Auto damage insurance appraisers, who compose 0.5 percent

Sales and related occupations make up 15.8 percent of employment. These include the following:

- Insurance sales agents, who compose 13.5 percent of all workers
- Supervisors/managers of sales workers, who compose 0.8 percent

The final 11.2 percent of employment in the insurance industry is in professional and related occupations. These include the following:

- Computer systems analysts, who compose 1.4 percent of all workers
- Computer software engineers, who compose 1.2 percent
- Registered nurses, who compose 1.1 percent
- Title examiners, who compose 1 percent
- Computer programmers, who compose 0.9 percent
- Computer support specialists, who compose 0.8 percent
- Actuaries, who compose 0.5 percent
- Market research analysts, who compose 0.5 percent
- Lawyers, who compose 0.5 percent

Medical service and health insurance is the fastest growing segment of the insurance industry, and despite increasingly expensive insurance premiums, significant growth is expected over the long term. As the baby boomers grow older and our nation's overall population reaches older ages than ever before, more people are expected to buy health insurance and long-term care insurance, as well as annuities and other types of pension products sometimes sold by insurance sales agents. If the Obama administration's legislation is enacted that makes health insurance affordable to more people, even greater increases in demand for coverage will result.

Population growth is stimulating demand for car insurance and homeowners insurance, as well as creating demand for businesses to service the needs of more people, and these businesses need insurance as well. In addition, growing numbers of individuals and businesses are purchasing liability insurance to protect against possible large liability awards from lawsuits brought by people claiming injury or damage from a product. Despite the fact that the Internet now allows many people to buy their policies online, thousands of job openings are still projected to arise in this large industry to replace the workers who leave or retire. That's because insurance clients still prefer to be face-to-face with sales agents to talk directly about policies, especially the more complicated ones.

Law

Legal issues will continue to arise in our society regardless of what the unemployment numbers are or where the Dow Jones stands. The legal system affects nearly every aspect of our lives, from buying a home to crossing the street, and that doesn't change in recessions or tight job markets. In fact, in some cases,

it becomes even more important to our daily lives. In tough times, when money is tight, people and businesses often turn to pursuing their legal options to make sure they're not getting ripped off, are receiving what they're due, or can safely and legally explore business options that can help save the life of a company. For this reason, and many others, law careers have remained consistent "Dow Busters," especially for the two occupations outlined in the following sections.

Attorneys

In good economies or bad, people are always going to need attorneys. While not every branch of law is recession-proof— real estate law, for example, has trouble weathering economic storms, especially when the housing market collapses as it did during our current recession—attorneys will generally continue to be in demand. Many practice areas can withstand economic downturns pretty well. Medical and health-care law is fairly stable because in a field that involves government programs and health insurance companies, poor economic situations lead to more disputes. Estate planning is strong, too, with people continuing to plan for the management and distribution of their assets after death no matter what the economic climate. The same goes for personal injury law. People don't put off litigation when they get hurt in a bad economy; in fact, more people pursue it.

I hate to say it, but the branch that's truly thriving right now is bankruptcy law. As you'd expect during one of the worst recessions in history, bankruptcy attorneys are busier than ever. Tough times mean that people lose their jobs and businesses go under, and bankruptcies increase as a result. Even when the current economy turns around, bankruptcy attorneys expect to remain busy to clean up the aftermath.

Another branch that's poised to take off is environmental law. You can expect to see that become a high-growth field as the nation invests more time and money in green energy and the environment.

There are about 761,000 attorneys employed in the United States (not including those who work as teachers in law schools), with employment numbers for the occupation as a whole expected to grow by 11 percent by 2016, adding 84,000 new jobs. Still, we can expect to see a greater job growth percentage in certain practices, such as the aforementioned bankruptcy and environmental law. Approximately 27 percent of lawyers are self-employed, working either as partners in law firms or in solo practices, while the rest tend to be employed by federal, state, and local governments, law firms, nonprofit organizations, and corporations like utilities, banks, insurance companies, and manufacturing firms. Most lawyers employed by the government work at the local level, such as district attorneys, while in the federal government they're employed mostly in the Departments of Justice, Treasury, and Defense.

Paralegals

Experiencing even greater growth in the law industry are the paralegals (also called legal assistants) who help attorneys in their work. There are 238,000 paralegals currently employed in the United States, with an expected growth of 22 percent by 2016, adding 53,000 new jobs. Private law firms employ 7 out of 10 paralegals, while most of the remainder worked for corporate legal departments and various levels of government, including the federal level, where paralegals are employed by the Department of Justice, the Social Security Administration, and the Department of the Treasury. Additionally, a very small

number of paralegals own their own businesses and work as freelance legal assistants, contracting their services to attorneys or corporate legal departments.

Employers are always trying to reduce costs and increase the availability and efficiency of legal services, and one way they're doing that, especially in a recession, is by hiring paralegals to perform the tasks once done by lawyers. As paralegals continue to take on a wider variety of duties, they become increasingly more useful to businesses. Community legal service programs, which provide assistance to the poor, elderly, minorities, and middle-income families, are also employing additional paralegals to minimize expenses while serving more people.

During recessions, corporations and individuals are more likely to face problems that require legal assistance, such as bankruptcies, foreclosures, and divorces. Because paralegals provide many of the same legal services as lawyers but at a lower cost, they tend to fare relatively better in difficult economic conditions.

Social Work

A sad fact of life is that times of intense financial stress may lead to more drinking, gambling, drug use, and domestic violence. Crisis counseling is always a steady source of employment, but during an economic recession, it becomes a true growth industry as more and more people seek help for stress and stress-induced behaviors. Accordingly, 4 of the 20 fastest-growing occupations in the BLS outlook are in social work, namely, substance abuse counselors, social services assistants, mental health counselors, and mental health and substance abuse social workers.

Social work employs roughly 595,000 workers. About 5 out of every 10 jobs in social work are in health-care and social assistance industries, and 3 out of 10 are employed by state and local government agencies, primarily in departments of health and human services. The industry's anticipated 22 percent employment growth reflects the importance that social work is taking on in our nation, especially during these difficult times. When we break the field down into its specialties, we can see even more evidence through the growth numbers of how vital this service has become:

- Mental health and substance abuse social workers are expected to grow by 30 percent, adding approximately 37,000 new jobs to the field.
- Medical and public health social workers by 24 percent, adding 30,000 new jobs.
- Child, family, gerontology and school social workers by 19 percent, adding 54,000 new jobs.
- All other social workers by 18 percent, adding 12,000 new jobs.

Job prospects in social work are excellent for workers who specialize in working with the elderly. The growing elderly population and the aging baby boomers are creating greater demand for health and social services, resulting in rapid job growth among gerontology social workers. The expanding senior population is also spurring demand for social workers in nursing homes, long-term care facilities, and hospices.

As substance abusers are increasingly placed into treatment programs instead of being sentenced to prison, social workers specializing in substance abuse are experiencing strong demand. More school social workers are in demand too as efforts are expanded to respond to rising student

enrollments and the continued emphasis on integrating disabled children into the general school population. Furthermore, as hospitals continue to limit the length of patient stays, social worker employment in home health-care services is picking up.

Employment of social workers in private social service agencies is also expected to increase. Employment in state and local government agencies is increasing in response to growing needs for public welfare, family services, and child protective services, though some services are contracted out to private social service agencies as well.

There are approximately 77,000 social service establishments in the private sector. Of that, 59,000 were in individual and family services; 9,000 in community food, housing, emergency, and other relief services; and 9,000 in job training. These establishments employ about 1.5 million workers, 65 percent of whom are in individual and family services. These social service agencies remain a great source of employment, posting an expected 54.8 percent employment increase by 2016, and you don't have to be a social worker to be employed there.

The service industry makes up 35.9 percent of employment in these establishments, with roles that include the following:

- Personal and home-care aides, who compose 15.5 percent of all workers
- Home health aides, who compose 8.2 percent
- Janitors and cleaners, who compose 2.1 percent
- Child care workers, who compose 1.7 percent
- Recreation workers, who compose 1.5 percent
- Nursing aides, orderlies and attendants, who compose 0.9 percent

- Residential advisors, who compose 0.7 percent
- Cooks, who compose 0.7 percent

An almost equal 35.4 percent of employment is in professional and related services. These include the following:

- Social service assistants, who compose 7.1 percent of all workers
- Child, family, and school social workers, who compose 4.1 percent
- Rehabilitation counselors, who compose 3.9 percent
- Mental health and substance abuse social workers, who compose 1.7 percent
- Educational, vocational, and school counselors, who compose 1.6 percent
- Teaching assistants, who compose 1.5 percent
- Mental health counselors, who compose 1.2 percent
- Registered nurses, who compose 1.1 percent
- Medical and public health social workers, who compose 1.1 percent
- Preschool teachers, who compose 1.1 percent
- Substance abuse and behavioral disorder counselors, who compose 0.9 percent
- Self-enrichment education teachers, who compose 0.8 percent
- Therapists, who compose 0.7 percent
- Health educators, who compose 0.7 percent
- Clinical, counseling, and school psychologists, who compose 0.6 percent
- Marriage and family therapists, who compose 0.6 percent
- Adult literacy, remedial education, and GED teachers and instructors, who compose 0.4 percent

Office and administrative support occupations make up 12 percent of employment. These include the following:

- Secretaries and administrative assistants, who compose 3 percent of all workers
- General office clerks, who compose 2.7 percent
- Bookkeeping, accounting, and auditing clerks, who compose 1.2 percent
- Receptionists and information clerks, who compose 1.2 percent

Next come the management, business, and financial occupations, which make up 8.8 percent of employment. These include the following:

- Social and community service managers, who compose 2.6 percent of all workers
- Human resources, training, and labor relations specialists, who compose 1.5 percent
- General and operations managers, who compose 1.3 percent

Transportation and material moving occupations make up the remaining 3.6 percent of employment. These include the following:

- Laborers and material movers, who make up 1.2 percent of all workers
- School bus drivers, who make up 0.9 percent
- Car drivers, who make up 0.7 percent

Some of the fastest growing occupations in the nation are concentrated in social services. The number of home health

aides within social service is projected to grow 79 percent by 2016, personal and home care also by 79 percent, and social service assistants by 76 percent, all primarily driven by the need to provide services to the elderly and ill in their homes who want to avoid expensive hospital or nursing home care.

Veterinary Medicine

Like the humans who own them, pets are living longer and receiving more advanced treatments for their ailments. It may sound strange to non-pet owners, especially at a time when so many people are having trouble taking care of just themselves, their spouses, and their children, but for many households, pets are considered valued members of the family. In some households, especially homes with only a single occupant, pets can even be elevated beyond "member of the family" status to that of a constant and faithful companion through thick and thin. In fact, pets are a major industry in the United States, with Americans spending $43 billion a year on the care and maintenance of their animal companions.

Because the majority of pet owners are relatively affluent, more people now than ever before are willing to pay for the advanced, intensive veterinary care that's available. Modern veterinary services have caught up to human medicine in a number of ways. Certain procedures, such as hip replacement, kidney transplants, and blood transfusions, which were once only available for humans, are now available for animals. Furthermore, the number of pet owners purchasing pet insurance is rising, indicating a growing likelihood and willingness on their part to spend considerable money on veterinary care.

Veterinarians

There are about 62,000 veterinarians currently employed in the nation. According to the American Veterinary Medical Association, roughly three out of every four veterinarians are employed in a solo or group private practice, while most of the others are employed in other fields. Data from the BLS show that the federal government employs about 1,400 civilian veterinarians, chiefly in the Departments of Agriculture, Health and Human Services, and, increasingly, Homeland Security, where bomb-sniffing dogs and other animals are used to perform security services. Other employers of veterinarians are state and local governments, colleges of veterinary medicine, zoos, aquariums, medical schools, research laboratories, animal food companies, and pharmaceutical companies.

Employment of veterinarians is expected to increase by an astounding 35 percent by 2016, adding 22,000 new jobs to the field. Not only is that a significantly higher percentage of job growth than most other occupations, it's higher than what is projected for registered nurses and pharmacists—the top two employment opportunities in health care for *humans!*

Because cats are increasingly becoming the pet of choice for today's busy lifestyle, faster growth of the cat population is bumping up the demand for feline medicine and veterinary services, while the demand for veterinary care for dogs continues to grow at a more modest pace. Continued support for public health, food and animal safety, national disease control programs, and biotech research on human health problems are also contributing to the demand for veterinarians. Homeland Security provides opportunities for veterinarians involved in efforts to maintain abundant food supplies and minimize animal diseases. Because most new veterinary graduates tend to go into pet medicine, preferring to deal with small animals and

to live and work near heavily populated areas, where most pet owners live, employment opportunities in rural settings are skyrocketing, especially for veterinarians trained in farm, ranch, and other large-animal care. Veterinarians with training in food safety and security, animal health and welfare, and public health and epidemiology will find themselves with the best opportunities for a career in the federal government.

Veterinary Technicians

Want to get in on all this veterinary medicine growth but can't or don't want to take the time to earn the four-year degree that's necessary? Then you're in luck because veterinary technologists and technicians, the people who assist veterinarians by conducting clinical work in a private practice under the supervision of a licensed veterinarian, are in even greater demand than veterinarians themselves. There are currently more than 70,000 vet techs employed, with the number of jobs expected to grow by 41 percent by 2016. That means 29,000 new jobs for this occupation that often requires a lot less training than veterinarians. Approximately 91 percent of vet techs work in veterinary services, while the remainder work in boarding kennels, animal shelters, stables, grooming salons, zoos, educational institutions, and federal, state, and local agencies. Biomedical facilities, diagnostic laboratories, wildlife facilities, humane societies, animal control facilities, drug or food manufacturing companies, and food safety inspection facilities also provide jobs for vet techs.

In the appendix, you'll find a comprehensive list of career resources for many of the roles and industries in this chapter, including certification courses, industry information and job sites, and information on how to apply for any related grants, scholarships, and loans.

MAKING THE TRANSITION: VETERINARY MEDICINE

Lena D., 29, of Seattle, Washington, works as a veterinarian at a low-cost animal health clinic, but the road that eventually led her there was a winding one—especially considering she had always wanted to be a writer. "I was studying for a master's in writing before deciding to go to vet school," she explains. "I love writing but didn't like the process of begging people to buy my work, in terms of making a living. I thought I would prefer people coming to me, instead of me going to them."

Though the roles of writer and veterinarian may seem worlds apart, it was actually Lena's graduate work in science writing that first sparked the idea. "I found myself very much enjoying writing about animal science and had had tentative plans for going to medical school. (For undergrad, I studied anthropology and pre-medicine. We didn't have any 'pre-vet' stuff, and at that time, I wanted to be a human doctor working abroad.) When I came up with the idea of vet school I knew right away it was the right thing—kind of a eureka moment." It helped that Lena, the proud owner of a 15-year-old dog and a 3-year-old cat, grew up around animals. "We always had a dog or two, and I had a series of pocket pets, fish, a bird, et cetera, in my high school menagerie. I also always loved horses and would ride every chance I got, which wasn't much." The economic implications of her decision to transition into veterinary medicine weren't lost on her either. "I did think I could make a better living as a vet than as a writer, but I also knew that vets make a lot less money than MDs."

After earning her master's degree in Science Writing from a university in Baltimore, Maryland, Lena began to explore her options for veterinary medicine programs. "I needed a few more prerequisites at the undergrad level, which I was able to take at a different university. I moved in with my parents to save money and spent $1,000 applying to 10 different schools. I had two interviews, got into three schools, and turned down a visit to a fourth. This is in line with the statistics; approximately

65 percent of people applying to a specific school don't get in. I think I would have been very happy at two of the schools I got into—it was nice to have a choice." She decided to attend a university in St. Paul, Minnesota, and began her four-year program in 2005.

"My parents had helped me pay for undergraduate, but I was on my own for my post-grad degrees," Lena explains about how she funded her education. "I was able to get work-study, scholarships, and grants for my master's program, but nothing like that was available for vet school. The entirety of my education, $175,000, was paid for through government loans, which I will be responsible for paying back at about $1,000 a month over the next 35 years." She considers herself one of the lucky students in that she managed to get a job before graduating. Still, she admits there were some difficult choices involved. "I ended up taking a job in a different city, half a country away from my boyfriend in Minnesota. I had also applied for an internship in emergency critical care, but given the time commitment—six days a week plus on call—and joke of a salary, I decided instead to accept a full-time general-practice position. I tried very hard to find a job in Minnesota, sending out over 20 résumés and interviewing at two jobs, one of which I was a finalist for. I didn't get a positive response from any of them. I flew out last minute to interview at the job here." She was offered the position in Seattle and found it provided a more reasonable work schedule than the critical care internship did. "I do get two days off a week, most weeks, and I don't have any on call, but I do work 10 to 11 hours daily, and my salary, as an associate this year, is a fraction of what the owners make. We are a *very* busy low-cost, walk-in clinic, which has not suffered many of the effects seen in other industries, which is why I think they were hiring." Lena believes it is the very nature of the clinic at which she works that has provided her with job security. "Because of the style of our practice, I really don't think there will ever be a danger of losing this job due to the economy. When times are good, many people are still living paycheck to paycheck and cannot afford the care at more traditional vet practices."

As a result, Lena is extremely satisfied with the work she does because it allows her to draw on both her love of animals and her desire to help people. "I especially like my current job because money is a big issue for my clients, and since I can provide services sometimes thousands of dollars less than they would cost at a specialty place, and they can afford to do it and save their pet's life, I really think that's valuable and I feel satisfied. Cheap vaccines—what a great public health idea! I do love the animals, of course, but I also love the mystery-solving aspect of medicine and the technical, almost artistic side of surgery. I do a lot of helping animals, but I think veterinary medicine is almost more about helping the owners sometimes."

For workers considering a career change into veterinary medicine, Lena says, "I guess the three basic qualities you have to have to be successful in vet med are: enjoy working with people, keep calm and focused in stressful situations, and have the ability to buckle down and work really hard—as in never sitting, skipping meals, and skipping sleep." If it sounds a lot like being a doctor for humans, that's because it is. "I've been a real vet for, oh, three months now, and just now am I getting used to the title of 'Doctor.'"

NEW DAY, NEW RULES

In the Introduction, I mentioned how the job market can seem pretty hopeless right now. With the national unemployment rate flirting with double digits, and some individual states well over that regrettable milestone, it's not hard to understand why. More people are out of work now than at any time in the past 26 years, and those who are lucky enough to still have jobs are seeing their benefits slashed, their hours cut back either through temporary furloughs or permanent changes, and more responsibilities put on their shoulders without commensurate pay increases as the jobs performed by their laid-off colleagues are redistributed among a shrinking workforce. I certainly can't blame the American labor force for experiencing low morale as we head into the next decade. Nobody could.

I'm hardly the only one who's noticed it. For example, back in May of 2009, an anonymous East Coast donor observed how the nation was reacting to the economic tailspin and immense job loss and decided to do something about it by starting an inspirational billboard campaign called "Recession 101." With some 2,000 postings across the country, and with all printing, materials, and billboard space donated by members of the Outdoor Advertising Association of America, the campaign is targeting particularly hard-hit states like Rhode Island, where unemployment has topped 12 percent, and Michigan, where it topped 15 percent. Among the slogans drivers can see peppered along the nation's roadsides are "Interesting fact about recessions . . . they end," "Self-worth is greater than net worth," and

my favorite, "This will end long before those who caused it are paroled." It's hard to put a lighthearted spin on the recession when people are worried about losing their jobs and homes, but keeping morale high is important.

It's just not enough.

With some 25 million people unemployed or underemployed, full job recovery is clearly going to take time, but as the mortgage bills come due, the savings accounts deplete, and the unemployment benefits run out, time is the one luxury no one has. Something needs to be done *now*.

I've already mentioned that because of the recession forcing a seismic shift from a manufacturing-based economy to a service-based one, most of the jobs that were lost aren't coming back, and, boy, is that a hard truth for workers to swallow. I see the anger, shock, and disbelief in people's faces all the time when I drop this news on them during my presentation, but the numbers bear it out. The automakers and other nondefense manufacturing industries aren't hiring people. In fact, they're letting more people go, even after restructuring and government bailouts. Unfortunately, businesses related to that sector are cratering along with them, such as car dealerships, where more than 3,000 establishments across the nation have closed, putting 100,000 employees out of work.

The industries that are still hiring are the ones that weren't hit all that hard to begin with, namely, the service industries. According to the BLS, service occupations are projected to have the largest number of total job openings, 12.2 million by 2016, with 60 percent of those openings coming from worker replacement needs alone as the baby-boomer generation heads toward retirement. Just take a look at the job growth numbers for the 18 highlighted in this book and you'll see what I'm talking about:

- *Health care.* 21.7 percent, or 3,000,000 new jobs created by 2016— the number one fastest growing industry in the nation
- *Biotechnology.* 24 percent, or 48,000 new jobs created by 2016
- *Education.* 3.5 percent, or 479,000 new jobs created by 2016
- *Green energy.* 25 percent, or up to 5,000,000 new jobs created by 2020

- *Government.* 4.8 percent, or nearly 1,000,000 new jobs created by 2016—the nation's largest employer
- *Security.* Hundreds of thousands of new jobs created by 2016 in both government and the private sector, including even more in classified departments and agencies whose numbers aren't made public
- *Information technology.* 24 percent, or 872,000 new jobs created by 2016
- *Entrepreneurship.* 6 million new businesses a year, 26 percent of the workforce turning to freelance and contract work, and independent niche consulting growing by 5.9 percent
- *Accounting.* 15 percent annually over the next decade, or 150,000 new jobs created every year
- *Customer service.* 25 percent, or 545,000 new jobs created by 2016
- *Dental hygiene.* 30 percent, or 50,000 new jobs created by 2016
- *Engineering.* A collective 11 percent, or 160,000 new jobs created by 2016
- *Finance.* 41 percent growth in personal financial advisors, or 72,000 new jobs created by 2016, and 34 percent growth in financial analysts, or 75,000 new jobs
- *Firefighting.* 12 percent, or 43,000 new jobs created by 2016
- *Insurance.* 7.4 percent, or 148,000 new jobs created by 2016
- *Law.* 11 percent growth in attorneys, or 84,000 new jobs created by 2016, and 22 percent growth in paralegals, or 53,000 new jobs
- *Social work.* A collective 22 percent, or 132,000 new jobs created by 2016
- *Veterinary medicine.* 35 percent growth in veterinarians, or 22,000 new jobs created by 2016, and 41 percent in vet techs, or 29,000 new jobs

Those are some impressive job growth numbers for the service sector, especially when you consider the alarming state of our national unemployment rate. In contrast, by June of 2009 the manufacturing sector had lost 1.9 million jobs because of the recession, while in the first quarter of 2009 industrial production fell at a 20 percent annual rate, the sharpest quarterly downturn of the current recession, and

the factory utilization rate dropped to 65.8 percent of capacity, the lowest percentage ever on records that date back to 1948.

The numbers are clear. If there's one single truth I want everyone who reads this book to come away with, it is this: *These jobs aren't coming back.* Not the same way.

Those industries deeply affected by the recession may not disappear altogether, but they're going to stay streamlined in order to remain competitive and, in some cases, because of dwindling demand for their products. That means these industries will focus on maintaining a lean workforce, not a robust one.

It's only natural to hold on to what we know and resist change. Humanity has been doing that for millennia, but as history keeps showing us, no amount of wishing and hoping can stop progress. Progress is what slammed the horse-drawn carriage industry when the first cars were manufactured. Progress is what shattered the typewriter manufacturers when word processing was born. As society's needs change and technology advances to meet those needs, certain industries and occupations get left behind and decline because of it. Whether or not that's fair is a moot point. It's like the end of the movie *Unforgiven*, when Clint Eastwood tells Gene Hackman that he may not deserve what's coming to him, but "deserve's got nothing to do with it." The kind of industry shift I'm talking about is simply a fact of life, one that workers need to accept if they don't want to find themselves trapped in a disappearing industry.

Look, Darth Vader couldn't beat Luke Skywalker, right? Tom couldn't beat Jerry. The coyote never beat the roadrunner. And workers are simply not going to beat the lessons of history by holding on to the dream of getting back the exact same jobs they lost. Think of it this way: You wouldn't show up to a computer system design firm looking for a job as a blacksmith, would you? You wouldn't show up to a telecommunications company looking for a job installing those big Bakelite rotary phones your parents and grandparents used, right? So why keep holding on to occupations that are going the way of the Model T?

We already know there's no job fairy who's going to come and magically change the situation so everyone can get back to work in

exactly the same jobs they used to have. It's time to stop waiting for a miracle and take control of your career. In order to get back to work quickly and with an eye toward lasting career stability, you have to go where the growth is.

Translating your existing skills into a new industry is not as hard as it appears. There's no reason an accountant from Lehman Brothers can't find another accounting position at a government agency, or a health-care establishment, or a university. Will the compensation be as much as what a Wall Street firm paid? Maybe not, but the salary will still be good, the job will be secure, you'll get your benefits back, and you'll have a solid retirement pension. The same goes for automakers and other workers laid off from a devastated manufacturing sector. Putting your existing skills to work in the manufacture of wind turbines or medical equipment instead of hoping car companies will start opening plants again can be the difference between losing your home and keeping it.

Learning a whole new skill can be more challenging than translating existing skills. Challenging, but not impossible. There are schools all over the nation that offer job training courses and professional degrees, many of which have convenient evening and online classes, and many of which offer extensive financial aid packages. There are also government-sponsored programs of little or no cost that exist specifically to train workers for the growth industries of the twenty-first century, including health care, education, IT, and green energy. On top of that, certain specific career occupations have grants that workers can apply for to help offset the cost of training. (You can find more information about schools and available grants for the industries discussed in the appendix.)

It's a whole new day out there, and in today's job market the old rules of job hunting and career management no longer apply. That means making big adjustments in order to get back to work. You simply can't afford to let the idea of learning a new skill hold you back. Besides, it's nowhere near as daunting as you might think. Certainly not as daunting as the prospect of losing your home, watching your retirement funds evaporate, and not being able to feed your family.

The American entrepreneurial spirit and work ethic is second to none, and even more so in times of crisis. If Bill Gates could create Microsoft during the recession of the 1970s, there's no reason why today's workers, who are more skilled and proficient than ever before, can't go on to achieve lucrative, lasting careers during a recession as well. It just means making some changes.

Recessions do end, just like the billboards say. But as the recovery continues to look like an increasingly jobless one, it's time to make the tough decisions about the next step in your career. With cutbacks, layoffs, and hiring freezes affecting almost every corner of the job market, it can be hard to know in which direction to take that step. That's where I hope *Where the Jobs Are Now* has helped. In the search for a lasting, stable career, you just have to know where to look, and not be afraid to make the change.

You'll be glad you did.

APPENDIX

This appendix is your one-stop resource and reference guide to all the industries, careers, and occupations mentioned in this book. Here you'll find links to online industry news and career information sites that will give you a well-rounded feel for the industry and provide access to cutting-edge news about the latest trends and employment needs. You'll also find links to the grants, scholarships, and loans available for the job training and certification courses that are sometimes necessary to make the jump into another field. Most of these courses are offered through convenient night, weekend, and online classes that can accommodate your schedule, as well as with helpful financial aid packages. Once you've chosen a school, though, make sure it is accredited for the field you're interested in entering. If it's not, your job opportunities could be severely limited despite your degree. Finally, you will find links to those all-important online job sites that are specifically tailored to each career or occupation.

Basically, this appendix is everything you could possibly need to explore, research, and take your first steps toward an exciting, lucrative, and, most importantly, stable new career.

Appendix Contents

Health Care

Industry News and Career Information

Academy of Managed Care   www.amcp.org/
  Pharmacy

AllNurses.com   allnurses.com/

AllNursingSchools.com   www.allnursingschools.com

American Academy of Nurse   www.aanp.org/
  Practitioners

American Academy of Physician   www.aapa.org/
  Assistants

American Association of Colleges www.aacn.nche.edu/
  of Nursing

American Association of Colleges www.aacp.org/
  of Pharmacy

American Association of Critical www.aacn.org/
  Care Nurses

American Association of   www.aamc.org/students/
  Medical Colleges

American College of Health-Care Administrators	achca.org/
American College of Health Care Executives	www.ache.org/
American College of Nurse-Midwives	www.midwife.org/
American Health Information Management Association	www.ahima.org/
American Medical Association: Careers in Health-Care	www.ama-assn.org/ama/pub/education-careers/careers-health-care.shtml
American Nurses Association	nursingworld.org/
American Pharmacists Association	www.pharmacist.com/
American Society of Health System Pharmacists	www.ashp.org/
American Society of Registered Nurses	www.asrn.org/
Association of University Programs in Health Administration	www.aupha.org/
BNET Healthcare	industry.bnet.com/healthcare/
Bureau of Labor Statistics: Emergency Medical Technicians and Paramedics	www.bls.gov/oco/ocos101.htm
Bureau of Labor Statistics: Healthcare	www.bls.gov/oco/cg/cgs035.htm
Bureau of Labor Statistics: Healthcare Jobs You Might Not Know About	www.bls.gov/opub/ooq/2008/summer/art03.pdf

Bureau of Labor Statistics: Medical and Health Services Managers	www.bls.gov/oco/ocos014.htm
Bureau of Labor Statistics: Medical Equipment Supplies and Manufacturing	www.bls.gov/oes/current/ naics4_339100.htm
Bureau of Labor Statistics: Nursing, Psychiatric and Home Health Aides	www.bls.gov/oco/ocos165.htm
Bureau of Labor Statistics: Personal and Home Care Aides	www.bls.gov/oco/ocos173.htm
Bureau of Labor Statistics: Pharmacists	www.bls.gov/oco/ocos079.htm
Bureau of Labor Statistics: Physician Assistants	www.bls.gov/oco/ocos081.htm
Bureau of Labor Statistics: Registered Nurses	www.bls.gov/oco/ocos083.htm
Career Voyages: Health-Care	www.careervoyages.gov/ healthcare-main.cfm
Center for Health Professionals	www.futurehealth.ucsf.edu/
Commission on Accreditation of Allied Health Education Programs: Profession Description and Certification Information	www.caahep.org/ Content.aspx?ID=19
Commission on Accreditation of Healthcare Management Education	www.cahme.org/
DiscoverNursing.com	www.discovernursing.com/
ExploreHealthCareCareers.org	www.explorehealthcareers. org/en/index.aspx

Fierce Healthcare	www.fiercehealthcare.com/
Healthcare Industry Today	health.einnews.com/
The Healthcare Intelligence Network	www.hin.com/
Health-Care Careers	www.health-carecareers.org/
HealthCareers.net	www.healthcareers.net/
The Medica: Health-Care Industry Overview	www.themedica.com/ industry-overview.html
Medical Group Management Association	www.mgma.com/
National Association for Home Care and Hospice	www.nahc.org/
National Association of Boards of Pharmacy	www.nabp.net/
National Association of Clinical Nurse Specialists	www.nacns.org/
National Association of Emergency Medical Technicians	www.naemt.org/
National Commission on Certification of Physician Assistants	www.nccpa.net/
National Council of State Boards of Nursing	https://www.ncsbn.org/ index.htm
National League for Nursing	www.nln.org/
National Registry of Emergency Medical Technicians	www.nremt.org/
Nursing Degree Guide	www.nursingdegreeguide.org

Pharmacy Week	www.pharmacyweek.com/
PhysicalTherapist.com	www.physicaltherapist.com/
Professional Association of Health Care Office Management	www.pahcom.com/
Visiting Nurses Association of America	vnaa.org/

Grants, Scholarships, and Loans

All Allied Health Schools	www.allalliedhealth schools.com/
American Health-Care Association: Scholarships	www.ahca.org/news/ nr030320.htm
Choose Nursing	www.choosenursing.com
CollegeScholarships.org: Healthcare Administration Scholarships	www.collegescholarships. org/scholarships/health/ administration.htm
Department of Health & Human Services Agency for Healthcare Research and Quality	www.ahrq.gov
The Department of Labor Employment and Training	www.doleta.gov/BRG/ IndProf/Health_grants.cfm
Discover Nursing Scholarships	www.discovernursing. com/scholarship_search.asp
My Online Nursing Degree/ Scholarship Resources	www.myonlinenursing degree.com/healthcare-scholarships.html
The National Health Service Corps	nhsc.hrsa.gov/
Nursing Scholarships	www.nursingscholarship. us/

PharmacySchools.com: Pharmacy Financial Aid and Scholarships	www.pharmacyschools. com/pharmacy-financial-aid-scholarships.html
Student Nurse Center	www.nursezone.com/ student_nurse_center/ Financial_assistance.asp
U.S. Department of Health and Human Services: Nursing Scholarship Program	bhpr.hrsa.gov/nursing/ scholarship/

Job Sites

Absolutely Health-Care	www.healthjobsusa.com/
AllHealthCareJobs.com	www.allhealthcarejobs.com
Careers in Health Management	www.healthmanagement-careers.org/
Health-Care Jobs	healthcarejobs.org/jobs.htm
Healthcare Jobs Online	www.hcjobsonline.com/
Health Career Web	www.healthcareerweb.com/jobs
Healthcare Source	www.healthcaresource.com
HealthJobSite.com	www.healthjobsite.com/
Hospital Pharmacy Jobs	www.hospitalpharmacy-jobs.com/Public/Index.aspx
MedHunting	www.medhunting.com/
MedJobScout	www.medjobscout.com/
Rx Career Center	www.rxcareercenter.com/
RXinsider	www.allpharmacyjobs.com/

Biotechnology

Biotech Industry News and Career Information

BioSpace	www.biospace.com/
Biotechnology Industry Organization	www.bio.org/
Biotechnology Institute	www.biotechinstitute.org/
Bureau of Labor Statistics: Pharmaceutical and Medicine Manufacturing	www.bls.gov/oco/cg/cgs009.htm
Career Voyages: Biotechnology	www.careervoyages.gov/ biotechnology-main.cfm
Council for Biotechnology Information	www.whybiotech.com/
FierceBiotech	www.fiercebiotech.com/
Fierce Pharma	www.fiercepharma.com/
International Biopharmaceutical Association	www.ibpaalliance.org/
Life Sciences World	www.lifesciencesworld.com/
National Center for Biotechnology Information	www.ncbi.nlm.nih.gov/
Pharmaceutical and Biotech Outlook	www.industrialinfo.com/ outlook_2009_pharm/demo/ index.jsp
Pharmaceutical Industry Channel: Jobs and Job Growth	www.imdiversity.com/ Villages/Channels/ pharmaceutical/pharma_ jobs_new.asp
Pharmaceutical Research and Manufacturers of America	www.phrma.org/

Science Daily's Biotechnology News   www.sciencedaily.com/
news/plants_animals/
biotechnology/

Science's ScienceCareers   sciencecareers.sciencemag.org/

U.S. Department of Labor: www.doleta.gov/BRG/
    Biotechnology Industry Profile   IndProf/Biotech_profile.cfm

U.S. Department of Labor: www.doleta.gov/BRG/
    Biotechnology Investments   IndProf/bioinvestment.cfm

Grants, Loans, and Scholarships

American Foundation for   www.afpenet.org/
    Pharmaceutical Education

CollegeScholarships.org: www.collegescholarships.
    Biotechnology Scholarships   org/scholarships/science/
biotech.htm

PhRMA Foundation   www.phrmafoundation.org/

Science's ScienceCareers: sciencecareers.sciencemag.
    Grants & Funding   org/funding

Job Sites

HireBio   www.hirebio.com/

HireRX   www.hirerx.com/

Lifesciencejobs.com   www.pharmajobs.com/

Medzilla   www.medzilla.com/

Pharmaceutical Crossing   www.pharmaceutical-
crossing.com/

PharmaOpportunities   www.pharma-
opportunities.com/

Education

Industry News and Career Information

Adult Student's Basic Guide to Online Learning: Job Outlook for Teachers	www.edpath.com/ GuidetoOL/job outlook teachers.html
American Association of School Administrators	www.aasa.org/
American Association of Colleges for Teacher Education	www.aacte.org/
America Association of Collegiate Registrars and Admissions Officers	www.aacrao.org/
American Council on Education	www.acenet.edu/
American Counseling Association	www.counseling.org/
American Federation of Teachers	www.aft.org/
American Library Association	www.ala.org
American School Counselor Association	www.schoolcounselor.org/
Association for Career and Technical Education	www.acteonline.org/
Association of American Colleges and Universities	www.aacu.org/
Association of Social Work Boards	www.aswb.org/
Bureau of Labor Statistics: Child Care Workers	www.bls.gov/oco/ocos170.htm
Bureau of Labor Statistics: Education Administrators	www.bls.gov/oco/ocos007.htm
Bureau of Labor Statistics: Educational Services	www.bls.gov/oco/cg/cgs034.htm

Bureau of Labor Statistics: Instructional Coordinators	www.bls.gov/oco/ocos269.htm
Bureau of Labor Statistics: School Athletic Coaches	www.bls.gov/oco/ocos251.htm
Bureau of Labor Statistics: School Bus Drivers	www.bls.gov/oes/ current/oes533022.htm
Bureau of Labor Statistics: School Counselors	www.bls.gov/oco/ocos067.htm
Bureau of Labor Statistics: School Librarians	www.bls.gov/oco/ocos068.htm
Bureau of Labor Statistics: School Social Workers	www.bls.gov/oco/ocos060.htm
Bureau of Labor Statistics: Teacher Assistants	www.bls.gov/oco/ocos153.htm
Bureau of Labor Statistics: Teachers K–12	www.bls.gov/oco/ocos069.htm
Bureau of Labor Statistics: Teachers Post-Secondary	www.bls.gov/oco/ocos066.htm
Bureau of Labor Statistics: Teachers—Adult Literacy and Remedial Education	www.bls.gov/oco/ocos289.htm
Bureau of Labor Statistics: Teachers—Self-Enrichment Education	www.bls.gov/oco/ocos064.htm
Bureau of Labor Statistics: Teachers—Special Education	www.bls.gov/oco/ocos070.htm
Center for Adult English Language Acquisition	www.cal.org/caela/
Certification Map	certificationmap.com/

Child Development Association Council for Professional Recognition	www.cdacouncil.org/
Chronicle of Higher Education	chronicle.com/
Council for Accreditation of Counseling and Related Educational Programs	www.cacrep.org/
Council for Advancement and Support of Education	www.case.org/
Council for Exceptional Children	www.cec.sped.org
Council of Graduate Schools	www.cgsnet.org/
Council on Social Work Education	www.cswe.org/
Directory of Schools: Online Education Degrees	www.directory-ofschools.com/
Education Industry Association	www.educationindustry.org/
Education Industry News	www.education-industrynews.com/
EducationNews.org	www.ednews.org/
Education Resources Information Center	www.eric.ed.gov/
Education Week	www.edweek.org/
Education World	www.education-world.com
Educause	www.educause.edu/
eSchoolNews	www.eschoolnews.com/
GreatTeacher.net	www.greatteacher.net/
InsideHigherEd	www.insidehighered.com

Making the Difference: Education Jobs in the Federal Government	www.makingthedifference. org/federalcareers/ education.shtml
NASPA—Student Affairs Administrators in Higher Education	www.naspa.org/
National Association for the Education of Young Children	www.naeyc.org/
National Association of Elementary School Principals	www.naesp.org/
National Association of Secondary School Principals	www.nassp.org/
National Association of Social Workers	www.socialworkers.org/
National Association of State Directors of Pupil Transportation Services	www.nasdpts.org/
National Board for Certified Counselors	www.nbcc.org/
National Board for Professional Teaching Standards	www.nbpts.org/
National Center for Alternative Certification	www.teach-now.org/
National Child Care Association	www.nccanet.org/
National Child Care Information Center	nccic.acf.hhs.gov/index.cfm
National Council for Accreditation of Teacher Education	www.ncate.org/
National Education Association	www.nea.org/

National Resource Center for Paraprofessionals	www.nrcpara.org/
National School Transportation Association	www.yellowbuses.org/
National Teacher Training Institute	www.thirteen.org/ edonline/ntti/
Personnel Center: Resource for Special Education Careers	www.personnelcenter.org/
Preparing Future Faculty	www.preparing-faculty.org/
Private School Review	www.privateschoolreview.com/
Public School Review	www.publicschoolreview.com/
Special Education News	www.specialednews.com/
Teacher Education Accreditation Council	www.teac.org/
Teachers' Network	www.teachnet.org/
Teachers.net	teachers.net/
TeachersCount	www.teacherscount.org/
University Business	www.universitybusiness.com
U.S. Department of Education	www.ed.gov/index.jhtml
U.S. Department of Education: Office of Vocational and Adult Education	www.ed.gov/about/ offices/list/ovae/index.html
Vocational Information Center: Early Childcare and Education Career Guide	www.khake.com/page15.html

Grants, Scholarships, and Loans

AFT: Loan Forgiveness Programs	www.aft.org/tools4teachers/loan-forgiveness.htm
All Education Schools: Teaching Scholarships	www.alleducationschools.com/faqs/scholarship
Council for Advancement and Support of Education: Awards and Scholarships	www.case.org/container.cfm?CONTAINERID=104&CRUMB=2&NAVID=67
CollegeDegrees.com: Teaching Scholarships	www.collegedegrees.com/financial-aid/scholarships/subject-based/teaching-scholarships/
CollegeScholarships.org: Teaching and Education Scholarships	www.collegescholarships.org/scholarships/teaching-students.htm
Educational Administration Scholarships	www.collegescholarships.org/scholarships/education/administration.htm
GrantsAlert	www.grantsalert.com/
National Board for Professional Teaching Standards: Scholarships	www.nbpts.org/become_a_candidate/fees_financial_support/scholarships
Online Education Database	oedb.org/scholarship/teacher
TEACH Grant Program	studentaid.ed.gov/PORTALSWebApp/students/english/TEACH.jsp
TeachersCount: National Scholarships	www.teacherscount.org/wannateach/scholarships/national.shtml

| TeachingTips.com: 101 Scholarships Just for Teachers | www.teachingtips.com/blog/2008/07/01/101-scholarships-just-for-teachers/ |
| U.S. Department of Education Grants and Contracts | www.ed.gov/fund/landing.jhtml |

Job Sites

Academic360	www.academic360.com/
Academic Employment Network	www.academploy.com/
Academic Position Network	www.apnjobs.com/
AERA Job Board	careers.aera.net/home/index.cfm?site_id=557
Chronicle of Higher Education: Jobs	chronicle.com/jobs/
Council for Advancement and Support of Education: Career Center	www.case.org/container.cfm?CONTAINERID=78&CRUMB=2&NAVID=62
EducationAmerica.net	www.educationamerica.net/
Educause: Job Opportunities	www.educause.edu/jobs?tid=16500
DeptofEd.org	www.deptofed.org/
DiverseJobs	www.diversejobs.net/
Edjoin	www.edjoin.org/
HigherEd Jobs	www.higheredjobs.com/
Jobsinschools.com	www.jobsinschools.com
k12jobs	k12jobs.com/
National School Applications Network	www.schoolapps.net/

Scholastic SchoolJobsNow	www.schooljobsnow.com/
SchoolSpring	www.schoolspring.com/
Teacher Job Center	jobs.teachers.net/
TeacherJobs	www.teacherjobs.com/
TedJob.com	www.tedjob.com/
TopSchoolJobs.org	www.topschooljobs.org/
University Business: Jobs	www.universitybusiness.com/viewjob.aspx
Wanttoteach.com	www.wanttoteach.com/

Green Energy

Industry News and Career Information

Agricultural Marketing Resource Center: Organic Food Trends Profile	www.agmrc.org/markets__industries/food/organic_food_trends_profile.cfm
American Academy of Environmental Engineers	www.aaee.net/
American Association of Blacks in Energy	www.aabe.org/
American Farmland Trust	www.farmland.org/
American Geological Institute	www.agiweb.org/
American Petroleum Institute	www.api.org/
American Public Gas Association	www.apga.org
American Public Power Association	www.appanet.org/
American Solar Energy Society	www.ases.org/
American Wind Energy Association	www.awea.org/

Berkeley Energy & Resources Collaborative: Career Guide for Energy, Climate & CleanTech Law	berc.berkeley.edu/ law-career-guide-temp
Bureau of Labor Statistics: Agriculture, Forestry and Fishing	www.bls.gov/oco/cg/cgs001.htm
Bureau of Labor Statistics: Careers in Energy	www.bls.gov/opub/ooq/ 2008/fall/art02.pdf
Bureau of Labor Statistics: Environmental Engineers	www.bls.gov/oes/ current/oes172081.htm
Bureau of Labor Statistics: Farmers, Ranchers and Agricultural Managers	www.bls.gov/oco/ocos176.htm
Bureau of Labor Statistics: Going Green	www.bls.gov/opub/ooq/ 2009/summer/art01.pdf
Bureau of Labor Statistics: Jobs for the Environment	www.bls.gov/oes/ highlight_environment.htm
Bureau of Labor Statistics: Mining, Oil and Gas	www.bls.gov/oco/cg/cgs004.htm
Bureau of Labor Statistics: Utilities	www.bls.gov/oco/cg/cgs018.htm
Center for Energy Workforce Development	www.cewd.org/
Discover Solar Energy	www.discoversolarenergy.com/
Edison Electric Institute	www.eei.org/
Energy Efficiency and Renewable Energy, Energy Education	www1.eere.energy.gov/ education/training.html
The Energy Foundation	www.ef.org/
Energy Information Administration	www.eia.doe.gov/

Energy Industry Today	energy.einnews.com/
Get Into Energy	www.getintoenergy.com/
Green Careers Guide	www.greencareersguide.com/
Green Energy Career Guide	www.greenenergyjobs. com/career-guide/
Green For All	www.greenforall.org/
National FFA Organization: Agricultural Education	www.ffa.org/
National Mining Association	www.nma.org/
National Sustainable Agriculture Information Service	attra.ncat.org/
Oil & Gas Journal	www.ogj.com/
Organic Agriculture	www.fao.org/organicag/ oa-home/en/
Renewable Energy World	www.renewableenergy- world.com/
Society for Range Management	www.rangelands.org/
Society of American Foresters	www.safnet.org/
SustainableBusiness.com	www.sustainablebusiness.com/
TreeHugger	www.treehugger.com
United Mine Workers of America	www.umwa.org/
U.S. Department of Agriculture: Cooperative State Research, Education and Extension Service	www.csrees.usda.gov/
U.S. Department of Agriculture: National Agricultural Library	www.nal.usda.gov/

U.S. Department of Agriculture: Family and Small Farms Program	www.csrees.usda.gov/familysmallfarms.cfm
U.S. Department of Energy	www.energy.gov/
U.S. Department of Energy: Energy Efficiency and Renewable Energy	www.eere.energy.gov/
U.S. Nuclear Regulatory Commission	www.nrc.gov/
Wet Feet: Energy and Utilities	www.wetfeet.com/Careers-and-Industries/Industries/Energy-and-Utilities.aspx

Grants, Scholarships, and Loans

American Association of Blacks in Energy: Scholarships	www.aabe.org/index.php?component=pages&id=4
Database of State Incentives for Renewables & Efficiency	www.dsireusa.org/
EcoIQ.com: Energy Scholarship and Funding Directory	www.ecoiq.com/onlineresources/directories/edtrain/scholarships/energy/index.html
Education for Sustainable Energy Development	www.e8.org/index.jsp?numPage=133
EnergyLoan	www.energyloan.net
Green Job Training Grants	greenjobtraininggrants.workforce3one.org/
Nuclear Energy Institute: Scholarships, Internships and Fellowships	www.nei.org/careersandeducation/educationandresources/scholarships/

Solar Energy Grants

www.alternate-energy-sources.com/solar-energy-grants.html

U.S. Department of Energy
Scholarships

undergraduate.eng.uci.edu/stories/storyReader$491

Job Sites

AlternativeEnergy.com

www.alternativeenergy.com/jobs

American Green Jobs

www.americangreenjobs.net/

CleanTech Jobs

www.cleantechrecruits.com/

Energy Crossing

www.energycrossing.com/

Energy Jobs Portal

www.EnergyJobsPortal.com

Energy Jobs Site

www.energyjobsites.com

EnvironmentalCareer.com

www.environmentalcareer.com/

Environmental Jobs and Careers

www.ecoemploy.com/

Green Dream Jobs

www.sustainablebusiness.com/jobs

Green Energy Jobs

www.greenenergyjobs.com/

Green Jobs Network

www.greenjobs.net/

Greenjobs

www.greenjobs.com

Professional Energy Jobs

www.professional-energyjobs.com/

Renewable Energy Jobs

www.renewableenergy-jobs.com/

SustainableBusiness.com	www.sustainablebusiness.com
Sustainable Industries	www.sustainable-industries.com/jobs
Think Energy Group	www.thinkenergygroup.com/

Government

Industry News and Career Information

About.com: Job Resources at Major U.S. Government Agencies	usgovinfo.about.com/bljobs.htm
Bureau of Labor Statistics: Federal Government	www.bls.gov/oco/cg/cgs041.htm
Bureau of Labor Statistics: How to Get a Job in the Federal Government	www.bls.gov/opub/ooq/2004/summer/art01.htm
Bureau of Labor Statistics: Postal Service Workers	www.bls.gov/oco/ocos141.htm
Bureau of Labor Statistics: State and Local Government	www.bls.gov/oco/cg/cgs042.htm
The Council of State Governments	www.csg.org/
International City/County Management Association	www.icma.org/
International Public Management Association for Human Resources	www.ipma-hr.org/
Partnership for Public Service	www.ourpublicservice.org/OPS/
Making the Difference	www.makingthedifference.org

U.S. Department of Labor:
  Employment and Training
  Administration

usgovinfo.about.com/gi/
dynamic/offsite.htm?site=
www.doleta.gov/

The U.S. Government's official
  Web portal

www.usa.gov/

Veterans Employment Information

www.opm.gov/veterans/

The Washington Post:
  "Government Careers"

www.washingtonpost.
com/wp-dyn/content/
discussion/2009/06/25/
DI2009062502851.html

Where the Jobs Are: Mission
  Critical Opportunities for
  America

www.ourpublicservice.
org/OPS/publications/
viewcontentdetails.php?id=118

Grants, Scholarships, and Loans

Experience.com: Government
  Fellowship Programs

www.experience.com/
alumnus/article?channel_id=
government&source_page=
home&article_id=article_
1142516799734

FedMoney

www.fedmoney.org/

Government Finance Officers
  Association: Scholarships

www.gfoa.org/index.php?
Itemid=107&id=96&option=
com_content&task=view

Johns Hopkins University:
  Government & Global Security
  Studies Internships/
  Fellowships/Scholarships

advanced.jhu.edu/
academic/government/
opportunities/

Studentjobs.gov: e-Scholar

www.studentjobs.gov/
e-scholar.asp

Job Sites

About.com: U.S. Government Job Finder	usgovinfo.about.com/ cs/jobs/a/jobfinder.htm
Careers in Government	www.careersingovernment.com/
Federal Jobs Digest	www.jobsfed.com/
Federal Jobs Network	federaljobs.net/
Government Job Finder	usgovinfo.about.com/cs/ jobs/a/jobfinder.htm
Government Jobs	www.govtjobs.com/
International Public Management Association for Human Resources	www.ipma-hr.org
International City/County Management Association	www.jobs.icma.org
Public Service Employee Network	www.pse-net.com/
State and Local Government Job Net	www.govtjob.net/
USAJOBS	www.usajobs.com/
U.S. Office of Personnel Management	www.opm.gov/

Security

Industry News and Career Information

Aerospace Industries Association	www.aia-aerospace.org/
All Career Schools: Corrections Programs	www.allcareerschools. com/search/all/all/Criminal Justice/corrections-officer/
All Career Schools: Criminal Investigations Programs	www.allcareerschools. com/search/all/all/Criminal Justice/criminal-investigations/

All Career Schools: Criminal Justice Programs	www.allcareerschools.com/ search/all/all/Criminal Justice/criminal-justice/
All Career Schools: Homeland Security Programs	www.allcareerschools. com/search/all/all/Criminal Justice/homeland-security programs/
All Career Schools: Law Enforcement Programs	www.allcareerschools. com/search/all/all/Criminal Justice/law-enforcement/
All Career Schools: Security Management Programs	www.allcareerschools.com/ search/all/all/Criminal Justice/security-management/
American Military University	www.amu.apus.edu/index.htm
ASIST International	www.asisonline.org/
ASIS International: Career Opportunities in Security	www.asisonline.org/ careercenter/careers2005.pdf
Bureau of Labor Statistics: Careers in Homeland Security	www.bls.gov/opub/ooq/ 2006/summer/art01.pdf
Bureau of Labor Statistics: Job Opportunities in the Armed Forces	www.bls.gov/oco/ocos249.htm
Bureau of Labor Statistics: Military Training for Civilian Careers	www.bls.gov/opub/ooq/ 2007/spring/art02.pdf
Bureau of Labor Statistics: Police and Detectives	www.bls.gov/oco/ocos160.htm
Bureau of Labor Statistics: Police Officer	www.bls.gov/k12/law01.htm

Bureau of Labor Statistics: Private Detectives and Investigators	www.bls.gov/oco/ocos157.htm
Bureau of Labor Statistics: Security Guards and Gaming Surveillance Officers	www.bls.gov/oco/ocos159.htm
Careers in National Defense	www.go-defense.com/
Criminal Justice USA	www.criminaljusticeusa. com/ins-agent.html
Central Intelligence Agency	www.cia.gov
Defense Intelligence Agency	www.dia.mil/
Degree Directory: Police Detective	degreedirectory.org/articles/ Police_Detective_Career_ Profile_Job_Outlook_and_ Education_Requirements.html
Federal Bureau of Investigation	www.fbi.gov
Federal Emergency Management Agency	www.fema.gov
Federation of American Scientists: U.S. Intelligence and Security Agencies	www.fas.org/irp/ official.html
International Council on Systems Engineering	www.incose.org/
Jobs Outlook: Police and Detectives	www.jobbankusa.com/ career_employment/police_ detectives/jobs_outlook.html
Library of Congress: Official U.S. Executive Branch Web Sites	www.loc.gov/rr/news/ fedgov.html
National Association of Legal Investigators	www.nalionline.org/

National Geo-Spatial Intelligence Agency	https://www1.nga.mil/Pages/Default.aspx
National Law Enforcement Recruiters Association	www.nlera.org/
National Security Agency	www.nsa.gov
National Sheriff's Association	www.sheriffs.org/
Nuclear Regulatory Commission	www.nrc.gov
Officer.com	www.officer.com/
Public Service	edu.public-service.us/
Police Magazine Industry Directory	www.policeonlinedirectory.com/
Transportation Security Administration	www.tsa.gov
U.S. Bureau of Alcohol, Tobacco and Firearms	www.atf.gov/
U.S. Coast Guard	www.uscg.mil/
U.S. Customs and Border Protection	www.cbo.gov
U.S. Department of Defense	www.defense.gov
U.S. Department of Homeland Security	www.dhs.gov/
U.S. Department of Justice	www.usdoj.gov
U.S. Department of State	www.state.gov/
U.S. Drug Enforcement Administration	www.usdoj.gov/dea/index.htm
U.S. Immigration and Customs Enforcement	www.ice.gov/
U.S. Marshals Service	www.usmarshals.gov/

U.S. Secret Service   www.secretservice.gov/join/

U.S. Securities and Exchange   www.sec.gov/
   Commission

Where the Jobs Are: Mission Critical   www.ourpublicservice.org/
   Opportunities for America   OPS/publications/
                                       viewcontentdetails.php?id=118

Grants, Scholarships, and Loans

College Scholarships.org: www.collegescholarships.
   Scholarships for Law   org/scholarships/
   Enforcement Students   law-enforcement.htm

Department of Homeland Security   www.dhs.gov/xopnbiz/grants/
   Grants

DHS Scholarship and Fellowship   www.orau.gov/dhsed/
   Program

Federal Grants Wire   www.federalgrantswire.com

Police Link   edu.policelink.com/

Ritchie Jennings Memorial   financialaid.syr.edu/
   Scholarship   scholar-ritchiejennings.htm

Security Job Sites

Aero Industry Jobs   www.aeroindustryjobs.com/

Aerospace and Defense Jobs   www.military.com/aerospace

Civilian Careers with the Air Force   ask.afpc.randolph.af.mil/

Civilian Careers with the Army   cpol.army.mil/

Civilian Careers with the Coast   www.uscg.mil/civilianhr/
   Guard

Civilian Careers with the Marines Corp	jobsearch.usajobs.opm.gov/a9usmc.aspx
Civilian Careers with the Navy	https://chart.donhr.navy.mil/
Clearance Jobs.com	www.clearancejobs.com
Cleared Connections.com	www.clearedconnections.com/
CopCareer.com	www.copcareer.com/
Defense Placements	www.defenseplacements.com/
The Defense Talent Network	www.defensetalent.com/
Department of Defense Jobs	federalgovernmentjobs.us/job-agency/department-of-defense.html
Department of Homeland Security Jobs	federalgovernmentjobs.us/job-agency/department-of-homeland-security.html
Federal Jobs Net: Law Enforcement Jobs	federaljobs.net/law.htm
GovJobs	www.govjobs.com/
Intelligence Careers	www.intelligencecareers.com/
JobMonkey.com: Law Enforcement Jobs	www.jobmonkey.com/lawenforcement/
JobsForUSCitizens.com	www.jobsforuscitizens.com/
Military Connection.com	www.militaryconnection.com/department-of-defense.html
Nation Job: Aviation Jobs/Aerospace Jobs/Defense Jobs	www.nationjob.com/aviation

Police Employment	www.policeemployment.com/
Police Jobs	www.policejobs.com/
PoliceOne.com	www.policeone.com/careers/
Security Job Zone	www.securityjobzone.com/
Today's Military: Careers	www.todaysmilitary.com/careers
Transportation Security Agency: Careers	www.tsa.gov/join/careers/
USA JOBS	www.usajobs.opm.gov/homeland.asp
U.S. Coast Guard	www.uscg.mil/top/careers.asp

Information Technology (IT)

Industry News and Career Information

Association for Computing Machinery	www.acm.org/
Association of Information Technology Professionals	www.aitp.org/
Bureau of Labor Statistics: Computer and Information Systems Managers	www.bls.gov/oco/ocos258.htm
Bureau of Labor Statistics: Computer Hardware Engineers	www.bls.gov/oes/current/oes172061.htm
Bureau of Labor Statistics: Computer Programmers	www.bls.gov/oco/ocos110.htm
Bureau of Labor Statistics: Computer Scientists and Database Administrators	www.bls.gov/oco/ocos042.htm

Bureau of Labor Statistics: Computer Software Engineers	www.bls.gov/oco/ocos267.htm
Bureau of Labor Statistics: Computer Support Specialists and System Administrators	www.bls.gov/oco/ocos268.htm
Bureau of Labor Statistics: Computer Systems Analysts	www.bls.gov/oco/ocos287.htm
Bureau of Labor Statistics: Data Entry & Information Processing Workers	www.bls.gov/oco/ocos155.htm
Bureau of Labor Statistics: Employment, Trends, and Training in Information Technology	www.bls.gov/opub/ooq/2009/spring/art04.pdf
Bureau of Labor Statistics: Internet Service Providers, Web Search Portals, and Data Processing Services	www.bls.gov/oco/cg/cgs055.htm
Bureau of Labor Statistics: Software Publishers	www.bls.gov/oco/cg/cgs051.htm
CBT Planet	www.cbtplanet.com/information_technology_courses.htm
CompTIA	www.comptia.org/
Computer Business Review	www.cbronline.com/
Computer Training and IT Certification Schools	www.compucert.com/
FierceWireless	www.fiercewireless.com/
Information Technology Council	www.itic.org/
Institute of Electrical and Electronics Engineers Computer Society	www2.computer.org/

IT Industry Today	it.einnews.com/
League of Professional System Administrators	lopsa.org/
National Workforce Center for Emerging Technologies	www.nwcet.org/
Software & Information Industry Association	www.siia.net/
University of Washington: Computer Science and Engineering	www.cs.washington.edu/ WhyCSE/
Wireless Association	www.ctia.org/
Wireless Week	www.wirelessweek.com/
Women in Technology	www.womenintechnology.org/

Grants, Scholarships, and Loans

Foundation for Information Technology Education	www.edfoundation.org/
National Science Foundation Scholarships in Science, Technology, Engineering, and Mathematics	www.nsf.gov/funding/ pgm_summ.jsp?pims_id=5257
CollegeScholarships.org: Software Engineers	www.collegescholarships. org/scholarships/technology/ software-engineering.htm
CollegeScholarships.org: Computer Programming:	www.collegescholarships. org/scholarships/technology/ computer-programming.htm
Google Anita Borg Memorial Scholarship	www.google.com/ anitaborg/

IBM Research Internship for Black, Hispanic and Native American Students	www.almaden.ibm.com/ almaden/diversity/
National Physical Science Consortium Graduate Fellowships	www.npsc.org/
Saludos Scholarships	www.saludos.com/ educationpavilion/scholarships/ compshl.html
Scholarships in Computer Science, Engineering and Technology	scholarships.fatomei.com/ engineering.html
Scholarships.com: Computer Science	www.scholarships.com/ computer-scholarships.aspx
U.S. Government Grants: IT	www.us-government grants.net/article_info.php/ articles_id/34

Job Sites

The Best International IT & Tech Jobs Online	www.iitjobs.com/
CityITjobs.net	www.cityitjobs.net/
DataProcessingJobs.com	www.dataprocessingjobs.com/
Dice	www.dice.com/
ITjobs.com	www.itjobs.com/
ITjobs.net	www.itjobs.net/
IT Jobs in Healthcare	www.meditjobs.com/
ITworld jobs	itjobs.itworld.com/
Jobs for Programmers	www.prgjobs.com/
Security Jobs Network	www.securityjobs.net/

Software engineer.com	www.softwareengineer.com/
Software Engineering Jobs	www.engineer.net/ software.php
Tech-Centric	www.tech-centric.net/
Tech Careers	www.techcareers.com/

Entrepreneurship

Industry News and Career Information

Abilities Fund	www.abilitiesfund.org/
About.com: Entrepreneurs	entrepreneurs.about.com/
About.com: Resources for Consultants	humanresources.about. com/od/consulting/Business_ Consulting_Management_ Consulting_Resources_for_ Consultants.htm
Accelerator	accelerator.eonetwork.org/ Pages/Default.aspx
America's Small Business Development Center Network	www.asbdc-us.org/
Association of Executive Search Consultants	www.aesc.org/
Association of Female Freelancers	shelancers.com/
Association of Management Consulting Firms	www.amcf.org/
BizStarters.com	www.bizstarters.com/
Bureau of Labor Statistics: Computer Scientists and Database Administrators	www.bls.gov/oco/ ocos042.htm

Bureau of Labor Statistics: Computer Support Specialists and Systems Administrators	www.bls.gov/oco/ocos268.htm
Bureau of Labor Statistics: Computer Systems Analysts	www.bls.gov/oco/ocos287.htm
Bureau of Labor Statistics: Environmental Scientists	www.bls.gov/oco/ocos050.htm
Bureau of Labor Statistics: Management, Scientific, and Technical Consulting Services	www.bls.gov/oco/cg/cgs037.htm
Bureau of Labor Statistics: Management Analysts	www.bls.gov/oco/ocos019.htm
Bureau of Labor Statistics: Profile of U.S. Data Sources on Entrepreneurship	www.oecd.org/dataoecd/24/46/37822254.pdf
Bureau of Labor Statistics: The Role of Entrepreneurship in U.S. and European Job Growth	www.bls.gov/opub/mlr/2000/07/art1full.pdf
Business Town	www.businesstown.com/
BusinessWeek: Small Business News	www.businessweek.com/smallbiz/
CNNMoney Small Business News	money.cnn.com/smallbusiness/
Coleman Foundation	www.colemanfoundation.org/
Collegiate Entrepreneurs Organization	www.c-e-o.org/
Consortium for Entrepreneurship Education	www.entre-ed.org/
Consultant Journal	www.consultantjournal.com/

Consulting Mentor	www.consultingmentor.com/
Consulting Pulse	www.consultingpulse.com/
DECA Inc.	www.deca.org/
Disabled Entrepreneurs Network	www.disabled-entrepreneurs.net/
Duct Tape Marketing	www.ducttapemarketing.com/
Edward Lowe Foundation	www.lowe.org/
Entrepreneur Career Guide	www.khake.com/page31.html
Entrepreneur.com	www.entrepreneur.com/
Entrepreneur's Journey	www.entrepreneurs-journey.com/
Entrepreneurs' Organization	www.eonetwork.org/
Entrepreneurship.org	www.entrepreneurship.org/
Forbes Entrepreneurs and Small Business News and Information	www.forbes.com/entrepreneurs/
Forum for Women Entrepreneurs	www.fwe.org/
Freelancers Union	www.freelancersunion.org/
Gaebler.com	www.gaebler.com/
Guerilla Marketing	www.gmarketing.com/
Inc.	www.inc.com/
Indus Entrepreneurs	www.tie.org/
Institute for the Study of Entrepreneurship and Management of Innovation	www.isemi.org/english/
Institute of Management Consultants	www.imcusa.org/

Internal Revenue Service: Starting a New Business	www.irs.gov/businesses/small/article/0,,id=99336,00.html
International Virtual Women's Chamber of Commerce	virtualwomen.groupsite.com/
Investment Management Consultants Association	www.imca.org/
Job Accommodation Network: Entrepreneurs	www.jan.wvu.edu/entre/
Kauffman Foundation	www.kauffman.org/
Kauffman Index of Entrepreneurial Activity	www.kauffman.org/uploadedFiles/kiea_042709.pdf
Management Consulted	managementconsulted.com/
Minority Business Development Agency	www.mbda.gov/
MoreBusiness.com	www.morebusiness.com/
MSNBC Small Business News	www.msnbc.msn.com/id/3627254/ns/business-small_business/
National Association for the Self-Employed	www.nase.org/
National Association of Women Business Owners	www.nawbo.org/
National Black Business Council	www.nbbc.org/
National Business Incubation Association	www.nbia.org/
National Federation of Independent Businesses	www.nfib.com/
New York Times Small Business News	www.nytimes.com/pages/business/smallbusiness/index.html

nPost Blog	www.npost.com/
Office of Disability Employment Policy: Entrepreneurship	www.dol.gov/odep/pubs/ misc/entrepre.htm
Office of Disability Employment Policy: Entrepreneurship Education	www.dol.gov/odep/pubs/ fact/entrepreneurship.htm
On Startups	onstartups.com/
Quicksprout: The Entrepreneur's Handbook	www.quicksprout.com/ 2009/05/10/the-internet-entrepreneurs-handbook-54-resources-for-first-time-entrepreneurs/
Quintessential Careers: Entrepreneur and Business Start-Up Tools and Resources	www.quintcareers.com/ entrepreneur_resources.html
Quintessential Careers: Job and Career Resources for Consultants, Freelancers and Gurus	www.quintcareers.com/ consultant_jobs.html
Resources for the Entrepreneur	web.mit.edu/ e-club/hadzima/
Service Corps of Retired Executives	www.score.org/
Small Business 3	www.smallbusiness3.com/
Small Business Administration	www.sba.gov/
Small Business and Entrepreneurship Resources	www.prenhall.com/ scarbzim/html/resource.html
Small Business Development Center Locator Map	www.sba.gov/aboutsba/ sbaprograms/sbdc/sbdclocator/ SBDC_LOCATOR.html
Small Business Knowledge Base	www.bizmove.com/

Small Business Solutions	www.whatspossible.com/
Small Business Trends	smallbiztrends.com/
SOHO America	www.soho.org/
Springwise	springwise.com/
Startup Nation	www.startupnation.com/
Start-Up USA	www.start-up-usa.org/
Social Venture Network	www.svn.org/
Tanned Feet	www.tannedfeet.com/
United States Association for Small Business and Entrepreneurship	usasbe.org/
U.S. Chamber of Commerce	www.uschamber.com/
Venture Hacks	venturehacks.com/
Wall Street Journal Small Business Marketing	online.wsj.com/public/ page/news-small-business-marketing.html
WomenPartner.com	womenpartner.com/
WorkHappy.net	www.workhappy.net/
Young Money	www.youngmoney.com/
ZeroMillion.com	www.zeromillion.com/

Grants, Scholarships, and Loans

About.com: State Sources for Small Business Grants	usgovinfo.about.com/od/ smallbusiness/a/stategrants.htm
Business.gov	www.business.gov/ finance/financing/
BusinessFinance.com	www.businessfinance.com/

Capital Connection	www.capitalconnection.com/
Go Big Network	www.gobignetwork.com/ funding/
Government Grants and Loans for Small Businesses	www.fedmoney.com/ grants/b0013.htm
Grants for Women in Business	www.womensnet.net/
Kauffman Foundation Grants	www.kauffman.org/ KauffmanGrants.aspx
Minority Business Grants	www.einfonews.com/
Small Business Administration Financing	www.sba.gov/services/ financialassistance/ Introsbafinance/index.html
Small Business Grants and Loans for Women Business Owners	www.womanowned.com/ growing/Funding/ Opportunities.aspx
Y Combinator	ycombinator.com/

Freelance and Consulting Job Sites

Accenture	accenture.jobs2web.com/
All Freelance Directory	www.allfreelance.com/
All Freelance Work	www.allfreelancework.com/
Aquent	aquent.us/
Bullhorn	www.bullhorn.com/
Contract Job Hunter	www.ceweekly.com/
Consultants on Demand	www.consultants-ondemand.com/
Consulting Crossing	www.consultingcrossing.com/

eLance.com	www.elance.com/
eWork.com	www.ework.com/
Flexjobs	www.flexjobs.com/
Freelance Job Search	www.freelancejobsearch.com/
Glocap Search	https://www.glocap.com/
GoFreelance.com	www.gofreelance.com/
Guru.com	www.guru.com/
Hireability	www.hireability.com/
I Can Freelance	www.icanfreelance.com/
Jobble	www.jobble.net/
KIT List	www.kitlist.org/
MBA GlobalNet	www.mbafreeagents.com/
Midbench	www.mindbench.com/
oDesk	www.odesk.com/
Robert Half Management Resources	www.roberthalfmr.com/ ConsultantResources
Smarter Work	www.smarterwork.com/
Solo Gig	www.sologig.com/

Dow Busters

Accounting Industry News and Career Information

AACSB Schools Accredited in Accounting	www.aacsb.edu/General/ InstLists.asp?lid=4
Accreditation Council for Accountancy and Taxation	www.acatcredentials.org/

Accounting Education Center	ceae.aicpa.org/
American Institute of Certified Public Accountants	www.aicpa.org/
American Women's Society of Certified Public Accountants	www.awscpa.org/
Association of Government Accountants	www.agacgfm.org/
Association of Latino Professionals in Finance and Accounting	www.alpfa.org/
Bureau of Labor Statistics: Accountants and Auditors	www.bls.gov/oco/ocos001.htm
Educational Foundation for Women in Accounting	www.efwa.org/
Institute of Internal Auditors	www.theiia.org/
Institute of Management Accountants	www.imanet.org/
National Association of Black Accountants	www.nabainc.org/
National Association of State Boards of Accountancy	www.nasba.org/
National Conference of CPA Practitioners	nccpap.org/
National Society of Accountants	www.nsacct.org/
Uniform CPA Examination	www.cpa-exam.org/

Customer Service Industry News and Career Information

Bureau of Labor Statistics: Customer Service Representatives	www.bls.gov/oco/ocos280.htm

Customers Are Always   www.customersarealways.com/

People to People Service   www.people2peopleservice.com/

Dental Hygiene Industry News and Career Information

American Dental Association   www.ada.org/

American Dental Hygienists   www.adha.org/
    Association

Bureau of Labor Statistics: www.bls.gov/oco/ocos097.htm
    Dental Hygienists

Engineering Industry News and Career Information

ABET-Accredited Engineering   www.abet.org/
    Programs

American Academy of   www.aaee.net/
    Environmental Engineers

American Indian Science and   www.aises.org/
    Engineering Society

American Society for Engineering   www.asee.org/
    Education

American Society of Civil Engineers   www.asce.org/

Biomedical Engineering Society   www.bmes.org/

Bureau of Labor Statistics: www.bls.gov/oco/ocos027.htm
    Engineers

Engineering Education Service   www.engineeringedu.com/
    Center

Institute of Industrial Engineers   www.iienet2.org/

Junior Engineering Technical Society   www.jets.org/

National Action Council for Minorities in Engineering — www.nacme.org/

National Council of Examiners of Engineering and Surveying — www.ncees.org/

National Society of Black Engineers — national.nsbe.org/

National Society of Professional Engineers — www.nspe.org/

Society of Women Engineers — societyofwomenengineers.swe.org/

Finance Industry News and Career Information

American Academy of Financial Management — www.aafm.us/

Association of Latino Professionals in Finance and Accounting — www.alpfa.org/

Bureau of Labor Statistics: Financial Analysts and Personal Financial Advisors — www.bls.gov/oco/ocos259.htm

Certified Financial Planner Board of Standards — www.cfp.net/

Chartered Financial Analyst Institute — www.cfainstitute.org/

Financial Industry Regulatory Authority — www.finra.org/

Financial Planning Association — www.fpanet.org/

Government Finance Officers Association — www.gfoa.org/

Investment Management Consultants Association — www.imca.org/

Life Office Management Association — www.loma.org/

Securities Industry and Financial Markets Association — www.sifma.org/

Firefighting Industry News and Career Information

Bureau of Labor Statistics: Fire Fighting Occupations	www.bls.gov/oco/ocos158.htm
International Association of Fire Chiefs Foundation	www.iafcf.org/
International Association of Fire Fighters	www.iaff.org/
National Fallen Firefighers Foundation	www.firehero.org/
National Fire Academy	www.usfa.dhs.gov/nfa/
National Fire Protection Association	www.nfpa.org/
National Volunteer Fire Council	www.nvfc.org/
U.S. Fire Administration	www.usfa.dhs.gov/

Insurance Industry News and Career Information

Actuarial Foundation	www.actuarialfoundation.org/
American Academy of Actuaries	www.actuary.org/
American Institute for Chartered Property Casualty Underwriters	www.aicpcu.org/
American Society of Pension Professionals and Actuaries	www.aspa.org/
Be an Actuary	www.BeAnActuary.org/
Bureau of Labor Statistics: Actuaries	www.bls.gov/oco/ocos041.htm
Bureau of Labor Statistics: Insurance	www.bls.gov/oco/cg/cgs028.htm

Bureau of Labor Statistics: Insurance Claims Adjusters, Appraisers, Examiners and Investigators	www.bls.gov/oco/ocos125.htm
Bureau of Labor Statistics: Insurance Sales Agents	www.bls.gov/oco/ocos118.htm
Bureau of Labor Statistics: Insurance Underwriters	www.bls.gov/oco/ocos026.htm
Casualty Actuarial Society	www.casact.org/
Chartered Property Casualty Underwriters Society	www.cpcusociety.org/
Classroom to Career Insurance Education	www.iiaba.net/eprise/ main/Invest/Index.html
Griffith Insurance Education Foundation	www.griffithfoundation.org/
Independent Automotive Damage Appraisers	www.iada.org/
Independent Insurance Agents and Brokers of America	www.iiaba.net/
Insurance Information Institute	www.iii.org/
International Association of Black Actuaries	blackactuaries.org/
International Claim Association	www.claim.org/
Life Office Management Association	www.loma.org/
National Association of Health Underwriters	www.nahu.org/
National Association of Professional Insurance Agents	www.pianet.org/
Property Casualty Insurance Association of America	www.pciaa.net/

Reinsurance Association of America   www.reinsurance.org/

Society of Actuaries   www.soa.org/

Law Industry News and Career Information

American Alliance of Paralegals   www.aapipara.org/

American Association for
    Paralegal Education   www.aafpe.org/

American Bar Association   www.abanet.org/

American Bar Association
    Standing Committee on
    Paralegals   www.abanet.org/
legalservices/paralegals/

Bureau of Labor Statistics: Lawyers   www.bls.gov/oco/ocos053.htm

Bureau of Labor Statistics:
    Paralegals and Legal Assistants   www.bls.gov/oco/ocos114.htm

Federal Circuit Bar Association   www.fedcirbar.org/

Latino Justice   www.prldef.org/

Law School Admission Council   www.lsac.org/

Mexican American Legal Defense
    and Educational Fund   www.maldef.org/

NAACP Legal Defense and
    Educational Fund   www.naacpldf.org

NALS Association for Legal
    Professionals   www.nals.org/

National Association for Legal
    Career Professionals   www.nalp.org/

National Association of Legal
    Assistants and Paralegals   www.nala.org/

National Black Law Students Association — www.nblsa.org/

National Federation of Paralegal Associations — www.paralegals.org/

Social Work Industry News and Career Information

Association of Social Work Boards — www.aswb.org/

Bureau of Labor Statistics: Mental Health and Substance Abuse Social Workers — www.bls.gov/oes/current/oes211023.htm

Bureau of Labor Statistics: Social and Human Services Assistants — www.bls.gov/oco/ocos059.htm

Bureau of Labor Statistics: Social Assistance — www.bls.gov/oco/cg/cgs040.htm

Bureau of Labor Statistics: Social Workers — www.bls.gov/oco/ocos060.htm

Council for Standards in Human Service Education — www.cshse.org/

Council on Social Work Education — www.cswe.org/

National Association of Social Workers — www.socialworkers.org/

National Association of Social Workers Foundation — www.naswfoundation.org/

National Human Services Assembly — www.nassembly.org/

National Organization for Human Services — www.nationalhuman-services.org/

Veterinary Medicine Industry News and Career Information

American Association for Laboratory Animal Science — www.aalas.org/

American Kennel Club	www.akc.org/
American Veterinary Medical Association	www.avma.org/
Association of American Veterinary Medical Colleges	www.aavmc.org/
Association for Women Veterinarians Foundation	www.vet.ksu.edu/AWV/ index.htm
Bureau of Labor Statistics: Veterinarians	www.bls.gov/oco/ocos076.htm
Bureau of Labor Statistics: Veterinary Technologists and Technicians	www.bls.gov/oco/ocos183.htm
Bureau of Labor Statistics: Wild Jobs with Wildlife	www.bls.gov/opub/ooq/ 2001/spring/art01.pdf
National Association of Veterinary Technicians in America	www.navta.net/
TLC Online	tlconline.org/
Western Veterinary Conference	www.wvc.org/

Accounting Grants, Scholarships, and Loans

American Institute of CPAs John L. Carey Scholarship Program	ceae.aicpa.org/Resources/ Scholarships+and+Awards/ John+L.+Carey+Scholarship+ Program.htm
American Institute of CPAs Scholarship for Minority Accounting Students	aicpa.org/members/div/ career/mini/smas.htm
American Institute of CPAs Student Scholarship	ceae.aicpa.org/Resources/ Scholarships+and+Awards/ AICPA+Accountemps+Student+ Scholarship+Program.htm

American Women's Society of CPAs List of Awards and Scholarships	www.awscpa.org/ frameset.php?cf=awards.htm
Association of Latino Professionals in Finance and Accounting Scholarships	alpfa.org/index.cfm? fuseaction=Page.viewPage& pageId=354
Business and Professional Women's Foundation Career Advancement Scholarship Program	financialaid.syr.edu/ scholar-careeradv.htm
Daniel Kovach Foundation Business Scholarship	financialaid.syr.edu/ scholar-dankovachbusiness.htm
Derek Hughes/NAPSLO Educational Foundation	financialaid.syr.edu/ scholar-derekhughes.htm
Educational Foundation for Women in Accounting Scholarships	www.efwa.org/ witwin.htm
F. Grant Waite, CPA, Memorial Scholarship	financialaid.syr.edu/ scholar-massachusettssociety.htm
Frank Greathouse Government Accounting Scholarship	financialaid.syr.edu/ scholar-frankgreathouse.htm
Forensic Accounting Scholarships	www.collegescholarships. org/scholarships/business/ forensic-accounting.htm
Michigan Accountancy Foundation Scholarships	www.michcpa.org/ Content/16284.aspx
Minorities in Government Finance Scholarship	www.gfoa.org/downloads/ 09MINORITIES_APP.pdf
National Association of Black Accountants Scholarship Program	www.nabainc.org/ NationalScholarshipProgramDraft/ tabid/370/Default.aspx

National Society of Accountants
  Scholarships

www.nsacct.org/
foundation.asp

New York Black MBA Scholarships

www.nyblackmba.org/
scholarship.html

Ritchie Jennings Memorial
  Scholarship

financialaid.syr.edu/
scholar-ritchiejennings.htm

Dental Hygiene Grants, Scholarships, and Loans

American Dental Association
  Grants and Scholarships

www.ada.org/ada/
adaf/grants/index.asp

American Dental Hygienists
  Association Scholarship Program

www.adha.org/institute/
Scholarship/

American Dental Hygienist
  Association Minority Scholarship

www.free–4u.com/
american5.htm

National Health Service Corps
  Loan Repayment Program

nhsc.hrsa.gov/
loanrepayment/

Texas Woman's University Dental
  Hygiene Finance Assistance

www.twu.edu/dental-
hygiene/financial-assistance.asp

Engineering Grants, Scholarships, and Loans

American Indian Science and
  Engineering Society
  Scholarships

www.aises.org/Programs/
ScholarshipsandInternships/
Scholarships

American Institute of Chemical
  Engineers Scholarships

www.aiche.org/students/
scholarships/index.aspx

American Society for Engineering
  Education Fellowships

www.asee.org/
fellowships/index.cfm

American Society of Civil
  Engineers Scholarships

content.asce.org/student/
scholarships.html

American Society of Naval Engineers Scholarships	www.navalengineers.org/ Programs/Scholarships/ Scholarship08_09.html
American Society of Heating, Refrigeration and Air-Conditioning Engineers Scholarships and Grants	www.ashrae.org/students/ page/704
American Society of Mechanical Engineers Scholarships	www.asme.org/ Education/College/FinancialAid/ Scholarships.cfm
ASM International Scholarships	asmcommunity. asminternational.org/portal/site/ www/Foundation/Students/ Scholarships/
Association for Iron and Steel Technology Foundation Scholarships	www.aistfoundation.org/ scholarships/scholarships.htm
Barry M. Goldwater Scholarship	www.act.org/goldwater/
Electrical and Computer Engineering Microelectronics Scholarship	www.eece.maine.edu/micro/
Engineering Information Foundation Grant Programs	www.eifgrants.org/
Engineering Vision Grant	www.engineeringvision.org/
Google Anita Borg Memorial Scholarship	www.google.com/anitaborg/
IBM Research Internship for Black, Hispanic and Native American Students	www.almaden.ibm.com/ almaden/diversity/
Institute of Industrial Engineering Scholarships and Fellowships	www.iienet2.org/ Details.aspx?id=857

MESA Engineering Program Scholarship	www.csuchico.edu/mesa/ mep_scholarship.shtml
Minerals, Metals and Materials Society Scholarships	www.tms.org/Students/ Scholarships.aspx
National Action Council for Minorities in Engineering Scholarships	www.nacmebacksme.org/ NBM.aspx?pageid=29
National Consortium for Graduate Degrees for Minorities in Engineering and Science	www.gemfellowship.org/
National Defense Science and Engineering Graduate Fellowship	ndseg.asee.org/
National Physical Science Consortium Graduate Fellowships	www.npsc.org/
National Society of Black Engineers Scholarships	national.nsbe.org/ Programs/Scholarships/ tabid/84/Default.aspx
National Society of Professional Engineers Scholarships	www.nspe.org/Students/ Resources/scholarships.html
Saludos Scholarships	www.saludos.com/ educationpavilion/scholarships/ compshl.html
Scholarships in Computer Science, Engineering and Technology	scholarships.fatomei.com/ engineering.html
Society for Automobile Engineers Awards, Scholarships and Loans	students.sae.org/awdscholar/
Society of Manufacturing Engineers Scholarships	www.sme.org/cgi-bin/ smeefhtml.pl?/foundation/ scholarships/fsfstudp.htm

Society of Women Engineers
   Scholarships

societyofwomenengineers.
swe.org/index.php?option=com_
content&task=view&id=
222&Itemid=229

United Engineering Foundation
   Grants

www.uefoundation.org/
grants.html

Zonta International Fellowships,
   Scholarships and Awards

www.zonta.org/site/
PageServer?pagename=
zi_scholarships

Finance Grants, Scholarships, and Loans

About.com: 10 Professional
   Groups That Offer Business
   School Scholarships

businessmajors.about.com/
od/payingforschool/a/
BusScholarships.htm

AllBusinessSchools.com:
   How to Pay for Business School

www.allbusinessschools.
com/faqs/financial-aid

Association of Latino Professionals
   in Finance and Accounting
   Scholarships

alpfa.org/index.cfm?
fuseaction=Page.viewPage&
pageId=354

Degree Directory Business Degree
   Scholarship

degreedirectory.org/
pages/business_scholarship.html

Derek Hughes/NAPSLO
   Educational Foundation

financialaid.syr.edu/
scholar-derekhughes.htm

Finance Scholarships

www.collegescholarships.
org/scholarships/business/
finance.htm

Financial Management Scholarships

www.collegescholarships.
org/scholarships/business/
financial-management.htm

Government Finance Officers
   Association Scholarships

www.gfoa.org/index.php?
option=com_content&task=
view&id=96&Itemid=107

Minorities in Government Finance Scholarship — www.gfoa.org/ downloads/09MINORITIES_ APP.pdf

National Business Association Scholarship Program — www.nationalbusiness. org/nbaweb/Member_Benefits/ E310.htm

New York Black MBA Scholarships — www.nyblackmba.org/ scholarship.html

Pace University Finance Scholarships — www.pace.edu/ page.cfm?doc_id=14037

Scholarships for Business Degree Concentrations — www.collegescholarships. org/scholarships/ business-students.htm

Straight Forward Media Business School Scholarship — www.straightforwardmedia. com/business-school/

Zonta International Women in Business Scholarships — www.zonta.org/site/ PageServer?pagename=zi_issues_ programs_klausman_application

Firefighting Grants, Scholarships, and Loans

International Association of Fire Chiefs Foundation Scholarships — www.iafcf.org/ Scholarship.htm

International Association of Fire Fighters Scholarships — www.iaff.org/et/ scholarships/index.asp

National Fallen Firefighers Foundation Educational Assistance — www.firehero.org/ index1.aspx?BD=7694

National Fire Protection Association Scholarships, Awards and Grants — www.nfpa.org/category List.asp?categoryID=205&URL= Learning/Training and professional development/Scholarships, awards, grants&cookie_test=1

National Volunteer Fire Council List of Scholarships	www.nvfc.org/page/ 1063/Scholarships.htm
NextStudent.com: Firefighter Scholarship List	www.nextstudent.com/ directory-of-scholarships/ corporation/0016/corporate- Firefighter-scholarships.aspx

Insurance Grants, Scholarships, and Loans

Actuarial Foundation Scholarships	www.actuarialfoundation. org/programs/actuarial/ scholarships.shtml
Be An Actuary: Scholarship Opportunities	www.beanactuary.org/ college/scholarships.cfm
CAS/SOA Diversity Exam Reimbursement Program	www.beanactuary.org/ diversity/waiver.cfm
Derek Hughes/NAPSLO Educational Foundation	financialaid.syr.edu/ scholar-derekhughes.htm
D.W. Simpson Actuarial Science Scholarship Program	www.actuaryjobs.com/ scholar.html
Insurance Scholarship Foundation of America	www.inssfa.org/ college.html
International Association of Black Actuaries Scholarships	blackactuaries.org/ actuary/scholarships.php
NextStudent.com: Actuarial Scholarships List	www.nextstudent.com/ directory-of-scholarships/Major/ 0122/Academic-Actuarial- scholarships.aspx
New York Black MBA Scholarships	www.nyblackmba.org/ scholarship.html
S.C. International Actuarial Science Scholarships	www.scinternational.com/ scholarship_application.asp

Law Grants, Scholarships, and Loans

AboutLawSchools.org: Law School Scholarships	www.aboutlawschools.org/law/career/scholarships/
Access Group	www.accessgroup.org/
American Bar Association Awards, Fellowships and Scholarships	www.abanet.org/yld/awards/home.shtml
CollegeScholarships.org: Paralegal Scholarships	www.collegescholarships.org/scholarships/law-enforcement/paralegal.htm
CollegeScholarships.org: Scholarships for Law Students	www.collegescholarships.org/scholarships/law-students.htm
Federal Circuit Bar Association Scholarship Series	www.fedcirbar.org/olc/pub/LVFC/cpages/misc/scholar.jsp
Foley & Lardner Minority Scholarship Fund	apps.foley.com/students/opportunities/minorityscholarships/
Law School Loans	www.lawschoolloans.com/articles/law-school-scholarships.php
Law School Vets	www.lawschoolvets.com/
Mexican American Legal Defense and Educational Fund Scholarships	www.maldef.org/leadership/scholarships/
NAACP Legal Defense and Educational Fund Scholarships	www.naacpldf.org/content.aspx?article=20
National Federation of Paralegal Associations Awards and Scholarships	www.paralegals.org/displaycommon.cfm?an=13
Puerto Rican Bar Association Scholarship Award	www.prldef.org/legal_education/scholarships.html

Sallie Mae Bar Study Loan	www.salliemae.com/ get_student_loan/find_student_ loan/grad/law_school_loans/ bar_study/bar_study_loan.htm
Sallie Mae LAWLOANS	www.salliemae.com/ im_applying/LAWLOANS_ Stafford_loan_checklist.htm
Straight Forward Media: Law School Scholarship	www.straightforwardmedia. com/law-school/
Yale Law School List of Outside Scholarships	www.law.yale.edu/admissions/ outsidescholarships.htm

Social Work Grants, Scholarships, and Loans

Association of Social Work Boards Research Grant Program	www.aswb.org/Links/ ResearchGrantProgram.asp
CollegeScholarships.org: Grants for Social Work Students	www.collegescholarships. org/grants/social.htm
CollegeScholarships.org: Scholarship Funding for Social Workers	www.collegescholarships. org/scholarships/ social-worker.htm
Council on Social Work Education Scholarships and Fellowships	www.cswe.org/CSWE/ scholarships/
National Association of Social Workers Foundation Fellowship, Scholarship and Research Awards	www.naswfoundation.org/ fellowships.asp
National Organization for Human Services Awards and Scholarships	www.nationalhuman- services.org/%5Btitle%5D-17

Veterinary Medicine Grants, Scholarships, and Loans

American Kennel Club Veterinary Technician Student Scholarships	www.akc.org/vetoutreach/ vt_scholarships.cfm
Association for Women Veterinarians Foundation Scholarships	www.vet.k-state.edu/awv/ scholarship.htm

Association of American Veterinary Medicine Colleges Scholarships	www.aavmc.org/students_ admissions/scholarships.htm
National Association of Veterinary Technicians in America Scholarship	navta.net/media/ WVC-NAVTA_Scholarship.pdf
NextStudent.com: Veterinary Scholarships List	www.nextstudent.com/ directory-of-scholarships/major/ 0200/academic-Veterinary-scholarships.aspx
State Veterinary Loan Repayment Program	www.avma.org/advocacy/ state/loan_repayment_programs/ default.asp
TLC Veterinary Scholarship	tlconline.org/pgm/0011.html
Veterinary Scholarship Trust of New England	veterinaryscholarshiptrust.org/
Western Veterinary Conference Scholarship Program	www.wvc.org/content/?c=44

Accounting Job Sites

A. E. Feldman Accounting Search Firm	www.aefeldman.com/ areas/accounting/
Accountancy Job	www.theaccountancyjob.com/
Accountant Careers	www.accountantcareers.com/
AccountantGigs.com	www.accountantgigs.com/
Accountemps	www.accountemps.com/
Accounting.com	www.accounting.com/
Accounting and Budget Federal Jobs	federalgovernmentjobs.us/ job-group/accounting-and-budget.html

Accounting Choices	www.accountingchoices.com/
Accounting Classifieds	www.accountingclassifieds.com/
Accounting Crossing	www.accountingcrossing.com/
Accounting Jobs Today	www.accountingjobstoday.com/
Accounting Now	www.accountingnow.com/
Accounting Principals	www.accountingprincipals.com/Jobs/
AccountingAssistant.net	www.accountingassistant.net/
AccountingCoach.com	jobs.accountingcoach.com/a/jobs/find-jobs
AccountingFinance.net	www.accountingfinance.net/
AccountingIntern.com	www.accountingintern.com/
AccountingSpecialist.net	www.accountingspecialist.net/
Accretive Solutions	www.cfoandcpajobs.com/
American Association of Finance and Accounting	www.aafa.com/
Childs, Smith & Associates	www.accounting-jobs.com/
CPAjobs.com	www.cpajobs.com/
D.C. Accounting Jobs	www.dcaccountingjobs.com/
Financial Job Bank	www.financialjobbank.com/
Financial Job Network	www.fjn.com/
KForce Finance and Accounting	www.kforce.com/

National Banking Network   www.nbn-jobs.com/home/
  Accounting Jobs   index.cfm

Samarak   www.samarak.com/

Customer Service Job Sites

Call Center Crossing   www.callcentercrossing.com/

CallCenterCareers.com   www.callcentercareers.com/

CSWork   www.cswork.com/

Customer Service Crossing   www.customerservice-
                               crossing.com/

Customers Are Always: www.customersarealways.
  Job Archives   com/customer_service_jobs/

CustomerHelpJobs.com   www.customerhelpjobs.com/

CustomerServiceAdministrative. www.customerservice-
  com   administrative.com/

CustomerServiceAssociate.net   www.customerservice-
                               associate.net/

CustomerServiceDataEntry.com   www.customerservice-
                               dataentry.com/

CustomerServiceJobs.com   www.customerservicejobs.com/

CustomerServiceJobSite.com   www.customerservice-
                               jobsite.com/

CustomerServiceRep.net   www.customerservicerep.net/

CustomerServiceRepresentative. www.customerservicere-
  net   presentative.net/

CustomerServiceSales.com	www.customerservicesales.com/
CustomerServiceSpecialist.com	www.customerservices-pecialist.com/
CustomerServiceWorld.com	www.ecustomerservice-world.com/ejobsstore.asp
iHire Customer Service	www.ihirecustomerservice.com/
TelephoneOperatorJobs.com	www.telephoneoperatorjobs.com/
TroyJobs.com	www.troyjobs.com/

Dental Hygiene Job Sites

Careers in Dental	www.careersindental.com/jobseekers.cfm
Dental Crossing	www.dentalcrossing.com/
DentalJob.org	www.dentaljob.org/
DentalPost.net	www.dentalpost.net/dental-jobs/DH/all-dental-hygienist-jobs
DentalWorkers.com	www.dentalworkers.com/employment/default.asp
Employment Crossing	www.employmentcrossing.com/lcjssearchresults.php?kid=2475&kwt=Hygienist&d=1578
Get Dental Hygienist Jobs	www.getdentalhygienistjobs.com/
Healthcare Jobs	www.healthcarejobs.org/
Health Career Web	www.healthcareerweb.com/jobs/search/?q=dental+hygienist
Health eCareers	www.healthecareers.com/jobs/dental

MedicalWorkforce.com   www.medicalworkforce.com/

My Dental Jobs   www.mydentaljobs.com/

Engineering Job Sites

American Society of Civil Engineers   careers.asce.org/search.cfm
   Career Connections

BestEngineeringJobs.com   www.bestengineeringjobs.com/

BioMedical Engineering   www.biomedicalengineer.com/

BioMedical Engineering Network   www.bmenet.org/BMEnet/
                                        db?action=list_by_keyword&
                                        keyword=job&ncolumns=1

Civil Engineer Crossing   www.civilengineering-
                                        crossing.com/

Civil Search International   www.csijobs.com/

CivilEngineeringCentral.com   jobs.civilengineering-
                                        central.com/JobSeeker/Jobs.aspx

CivilEngineeringJobs.com   www.civilengineeringjobs.com/

ECEA Jobs Online   www.eceajobs.com/

Engineer Jobs   www.engineer-jobs.com/

Engineer.net   www.engineer.net/

Engineering Careers Online   www.engineeringcareers-
                                        online.com/

Engineering Central   www.engcen.com/

Engineering Classifieds   www.engineering-
                                        classifieds.com/

Engineering Crossing   www.engineering-
                                        crossing.com/

Engineering Job Site	www.engineering-job-site.com/
Engineering Network	www.engnetglobal.com/jobs/engineering_jobs.aspx
Engineering Resource Group	www.engineeringresource.com/
Engineering.com Job Listings	www.engineering.com/Jobs/tabid/5120/Default.aspx
EngineeringJobs.com	www.engineerjobs.com/
EngineeringJobs.net	www.engineeringjobs.net/
Environmental Engineer	www.environmental-engineer.com/
Environmental Engineering Jobs	www.environmentaljobs.com/environmental-engineering-jobs.htm
Go 4 Engineering Jobs	www.go4engineeringjobs.com/
Graduating Engineer	www.graduatingengineer.com/
iCivil Engineer	www.icivilengineer.com/Jobs/
iHire Engineering	www.ihireengineering.com/
Industrial Engineer	www.industrialengineer.com/
Institute of Industrial Engineering Career Center	www.iienet2.org/Landing.aspx?id=388
Internet Engineering Center	www.interec.net/
National Engineering Resources	www.nerinc.com/
Recruiters on the Net Engineering, Manufacturing and Technical Jobs	www.recruitersonthenet.com/

SAEJob.com	www.saejob.com/
TechCareers	www.techcareers.com/
Think Energy Group	www.thinkenergygroup.com/

Finance Job Sites

AccountantFinancialAnalyst.com	www.accountantfinancial-analyst.com/
Accounting and Budget Federal Jobs	federalgovernmentjobs.us/job-group/accounting-and-budget.html
Accounting Career Network	www.searchaccountingjobs.com/
Accounting Now	www.accountingnow.com/
Accounting Principals	www.accountingprincipals.com/Jobs/
American Academy of Financial Management Job Board	www.financialanalyst.org/jobsfinance.html
American Association of Finance and Accounting Search Specialists	www.aafa.com/
BrokerHunter.com	www.brokerhunter.com/
Careers-in-Finance	www.careers-in-finance.com/
Closers.net	www.closers.net/
CPAjobs.com	www.cpajobs.com/
D.C. Accounting Jobs	www.dcaccountingjobs.com/
eFinancial Careers	www.efinancialcareers.com/

EntryLevelFinancialAnalyst.com	www.entrylevelfinancial-analyst.com/
Finance Job	www.thefinancejob.com/
Finance Jobs	www.expatfinancejobs.com/
Financial Job Bank	www.financialjobbank.com/
Financial Job Network	www.fjn.com/
Financial Jobs	www.financial-jobs-search.com/
Financial Positions	www.financialpositions.com/
Financial Services Crossing	www.financialservices-crossing.com/
FinancialAdvisorJobs.net	www.financialadvisorjobs.net/
FinancialJobs.com	www.financialjobs.com/
FinCareer	www.fincareer.com/
Fins	www.fins.com/Finance/Jobs
Get Financial Analyst Jobs	www.getfinancial-analystjobs.com/
iHire Finance	www.ihirefinance.com/
InvestmentPositions.com	www.investmentpositions.com/
Jobs in the Money	www.jobsinthemoney.com/
KForce Finance and Accounting	www.Kforce.com/
National Banking Network Finance Jobs	www.nbn-jobs.com/
Robert Half Finance and Accounting	www.roberthalffinance.com/
Vault	www.vault.com/

Firefighting Job Sites

EMSFireRescueJobs.com	www.emsfirerescuejobs.com/
Fire Career Assistance	www.firecareerassist.com/
Fire Link	www.firelink.com/careers
Fire Rescue 1	www.firerescue1.com/fire-jobs/
FireCareers.com	www.firecareers.com/
Firefighter Jobs	www.firefighter-jobs.com/
Firefighter Nation.com	jobs.firefighternation.com/a/jbb/find-jobs
FireHire Inc.	www.firehire.com/
Firehouse.com	cms.firehouse.com/content/jobs/
Firejobs	www.firejobs.com/
Firemen Jobs	www.firemenjobs.com/
FireRecruit.com	www.firerecruit.com/
National Park Service Fire Jobs	www.nps.gov/fire/employment/emp_jobsearch.cfm
U.S. Department of the Interior Fire Jobs	www.firejobs.doi.gov/
U.S. Forest Service Fire Jobs	www.fs.fed.us/eacc/library/docs/jobs.shtml
Wildland Fire	www.wildlandfire.com/jobs.htm

Insurance Job Sites

4 Insurance Jobs	www.4insurancejobs.com/
Actuarial Careers Inc.	www.actuarialcareers.com/

Actuary.com	www.actuary.com/
ActuaryJobsite.com	www.actuaryjobsite.com/
AdjusterJobs.com	www.adjusterjobs.com/
AdjusterJobsite.com	www.adjusterjobsite.com/
Careers-in-Finance: Insurance	www.careers-in-finance.com/in.htm
Closers.net	www.closers.net/
D.W. Simpson Global Actuarial Recruitment	www.actuaryjobs.com/
Great Insurance Jobs	www.greatinsurancejobs.com/
Great Insurance Recruiters	www.greatinsurancerecruiters.com/
iHire Insurance	www.ihireinsurance.com/
Insurance Crossing	www.insurcrossing.com/
Insurance Job Channel	www.insurancejobchannel.com/
Insurance Jobs Center	insurance-jobs-center.com/
Insurance Personnel Resources	www.insurancepersonnel.net/
Insurance Sales Jobs	www.insurancesalesjobs.com/
InsuranceCareer.com	www.insurancecareer.com/
InsuranceCareerSite.com	www.insurancecareersite.com/
InsuranceClaimsWeb.com	www.insuranceclaimsweb.com/
InsuranceJobs.com	www.insurancejobs.com/
InsuranceUnderwritingWeb.com	www.insuranceunderwritingweb.com/

InsuranceWorkforce.com	www.insuranceworkforce.com/
InsuranceWorkforce.net	www.insuranceworkforce.net/
InsuranceWorks.com	www.insuranceworks.com/
Jobs4Actuary.com	jobs4actuary.com/
National Insurance Recruiters Association	www.nirassn.com/
Society of Actuaries Job Board	jobs.soa.org/
Ultimate Insurance Jobs	www.ultimateinsurancejobs. com/index.asp
UnderwritingJobs.com	www.underwritingjobs.com/

Law Job Sites

All Law Job Resources	www.alllaw.com/ legal_practice_information/jobs/
Attorney Jobs	www.attorneyjobs.com/
AttorneyJobsite.com	www.attorneyjobsite.com/
Counsel.net Attorney Network	counsel.net/jobs/
EmplawyerNet	www.emplawyernet.com/
Federal Government Legal Jobs	federalgovernmentjobs.us/ job-group/legal-and-kindred.html
Federal Legal Jobs	www.jobsfed.com/ GroupDet10.htm
HG.org Worldwide Legal Directories	www.hg.org/law-jobs.asp
iHire Legal	www.ihirelegal.com/
InsuranceLawJobs.com	www.insurancelawjobs.com/

Juris Resources	www.jurisresources.com/
Law Career Center	careers.findlaw.com/
Law Crossing	www.lawcrossing.com/
Law Firm Staff	www.lawfirmstaff.com/
Law Network Job Board	www.thelaw.com/jobs/
Lawguru.com Career Center	lawguru.legalstaff.com/ Common/HomePage.aspx?abbr= LAWGURU
LawInfo Career Center	jobs.lawinfo.com/
Lawjobs.com	www.lawjobs.com/
Legal Authority	www.legalauthority.com/
Legal Job	www.thelegaljob.com/
LegalCareerSite	www.legalcareersite.com/
LegalJob.org	www.legaljob.org/
National Federation of Paralegal Associations Career Center	paralegals.legalstaff.com/
Paralegal Job Finder	www.paralegaljobfinder.com/
ParalegalJobs.com	www.paralegaljobs.com/
Staffing Now Legal Services	www.staffingnow.com/ staffing-services/legal.php
U.S. Department of Justice Attorney Vacancies	www.usdoj.gov/oarm/ attvacancies.html

Social Work Job Sites

Council on Social Work Education Career Center	careers.cswe.org/home/ index.cfm?site_id=392
eCarers	www.ecarers.com/

Federal Government Social Worker Jobs	federalgovernmentjobs.us/ job-search/social-worker–0185. html
Healthcare Jobs: Health and Social Service Jobs	www.healthcarejobs.org/ hsso.htm
Human Services Career Network	www.hscareers.com/
iHire Health and Social	www.ihirehealthandsocial.com/
iHire Social Services	www.ihiresocialservices.com/
Jobs for Social Workers	www.jobsforsocialworkers.com/
MedHunting.com Social Work Jobs	www.medhunting.com/ social-work-jobs.htm
MedicalWorkers.com: Social Worker Jobs	www.medicalworkers.com/ employment/social-worker-msw- jobs.aspx
Social Work Career Center	careers.socialworkers.org/
Social Work Job Bank	www.socialworkjobbank.com/
Social Work Job Search	www.friedsocialworker. com/CareerResources/ socialworkjobs.htm
Social Work Jobs	www.socialworkjobs.com/
Social Work Search	www.socialworksearch. com/cgi/socialwork.cgi?search= CAT&Category=Websites: Employment+Opportunities
SocialService.com	www.socialservice.com/
SocialServiceNetwork.com	socialservicenetwork.com/
SocialWork.com	www.socialwork.com/

Veterinary Medicine Job Sites

American Veterinary Medicine Career Center — www.avma.org/vcc/default.asp

AnimalWork.com — www.animalwork.com/

ASPCA Job Board — www.aspca.org/about-us/jobs/

Association of American Veterinary Medical Colleges Career Center — jobs.aavmc.org/

Health-Care Hiring: Veterinarian Jobs — healthcarehiring.jobamatic.com/a/jobs/find-jobs/q-veterinarian

Health-Care Hiring: Veterinary — healthcarehiring.jobamatic.com/a/jobs/find-jobs/q-veterinary+tech

iHire Veterinary — www.ihireveterinary.com/

iHire Veterinary: Veterinary Technician Jobs — www.ihireveterinary.com/t-Veterinary-Technician-jobs.html

National Association of Veterinary Technicians in America Career Center — www.navta.net/index.php?pr=Career_Center

VCA Veterinary Clinics Jobs — www.vcapets.com/career/veterinary-clinic-jobs.asp

Vet Broker — www.vetbroker.com/

Vet Classifieds — www.vetclassifieds.com/

Vet Recruiter — www.thevetrecruiter.com/

Veterinary and Animal Health Jobs — bestvetstore.com/vetjobs/

Veterinary Crossing — www.veterinarycrossing.com/

Veterinary Jobs Marketplace Service — www.jobs.vetclinics.net/

Veterinary Tech Jobs — www.veterinarytechjobs.com/

VeterinaryJobs.com   www.veterinaryjobs.com/

WhereTechsConnect.com   www.wheretechsconnect.com/

General Job Info

General Company Information Sites

Corporate Information   www.corporateinformation.com/

Hoover's   www.hoovers.com

Industry Portals/Industry Hubs   www.virtualpet.com/
                                         industry/mfg/mfg.htm

Specialissues.com: List of Lists   www.specialissues.com/lol/

Yahoo Industry News   biz.yahoo.com/industry/

General Career Sites

About.com Career Planning Guide   careerplanning.about.com/

Bureau of Labor Statistics: www.bls.gov/oco/
   Occupational Outlook Handbook

Career Overview   www.careeroverview.com/

Career Voyages   www.careervoyages.gov/

CollegeGrad's Top 30 Careers   www.collegegrad.com/
                                         careers/

Job Diagnosis   www.Jobdiagnosis.com

JobWeb   www.jobweb.com/

Vault.com   www.vault.com/

Wall Street Journal: Careers   online.wsj.com/public/
                                         page/news-career-jobs.html

General Job Sites

About.com	jobsearch.about.com/
Beyond.com	www.beyond.com/
Career Builder	www.careerbuilder.com
Career One Stop Service Locator	www.servicelocator.org/
Craigslist	www.craigslist.org
The ExecuSearch Group	www.execu-search.com/
Hound	www.hound.com/
Idealist.org	www.idealist.org/
Indeed	www.indeed.com/
Jobster	www.jobster.com/
Juju	www.job-searchengine.com/
Latino-Bilingual Employment Opportunities	latcareers.com/
LinkedIn	www.linkedin.com
Linkup	www.linkup.com
Monster	www.monster.com
Oodle	www.oodle.com/job/
Searchline Professional/ Executive Search	www.searchlinejobs.com/
Simply Hired	www.simplyhired.com/
Snag a Job	www.snagajob.com/
Worktree	www.worktree.com
Yahoo Hotjobs	hotjobs.yahoo.com

INDEX

ABOUT THE AUTHOR

Joe Watson is a nationally recognized author, media personality, public speaker and business leader. He is currently the CEO of Without Excuses and StrategicHire, located in Reston, VA.

His expert opinion is highly valued by the national media. Mr. Watson has provided frequent analysis on leading national television shows such as **The Today Show, CBS Early Show, CNN, FOX News and PBS**; and he has been heard on numerous radio stations throughout the country, including XM Satellite, Sirius, Fox News, and CBS Market Watch etc. Mr. Watson has provided analysis in many print publications, including The New York Times, The Wall Street Journal, The Washington Post, USA Today, Essence Magazine, International Herald Tribune, The Chronicle of Philanthropy, Fast Company and Black Enterprise amongst many others.

Mr. Watson's book – *"Where The Jobs Are Now"* was published by **McGraw-Hill**. His previous book – *"Without Excuses"* was published by **St. Martin's Press** in 2006.

He is a nationally known speaker and strategic advisor to a diverse array of organizations, individuals and corporations. A sampling includes: Traveler's Insurance, Rockefeller Foundation, The Creative Economy Conference/ Fortune Magazine, MetLife, NOVA University Franchise CEO Summit, AXA Equitable,

Sodexho USA, Society for Human Resource Management, Diversity Best Practices, The Executive Leadership Council, MTV Networks, Wall Street Summit, NAMIC, NABA, Sallie Mae and many others.

Mr. Watson is Chairman of **The Marathon Club** (www.themarathonclub.org) - a leading National group focused on driving wealth creation for entrepreneurs and private equity firms. The Marathon Club's 1,000+ members consists of private equity firms which manage funds in excess of **$11 billion**, over (450) Fortune 500 members within two levels of the CEO, and numerous large business owners, Partner level professional services representatives and other extended business alliances.

He is an Advisor to The Executive Leadership Council. Member, the National Board of Directors for The Congressional Award Foundation, Advisory Board Member, former Chairman of the Greater Reston Chamber of Commerce and also, sits on the Boards of several other commercial and non-profit entities.

Mr. Watson is a passionate advocate for progress though excellence and truth. His personal slogan for success is "Subtle Pressure, Relentlessly Applied".

Please visit Joe at www.WhereTheJobsAreNow.com and www.WithoutExcuses.com

A Reel on Mr. Watson can be accessed by visiting – http://www.gearshift.tv/video/joewatson_demo2008.wmv